TRUTHFORLIFE®
THE BIBLE-TEACHING MINISTRY OF **ALISTAIR BEGG**

The mission of Truth For Life is to teach the Bible with clarity and relevance so that unbelievers will be converted, believers will be established, and local churches will be strengthened.

Daily Program
Each day, Truth For Life distributes the Bible teaching of Alistair Begg across the U.S. and in several locations outside of the U.S. through 2,000 radio outlets. To find a radio station near you, visit **truthforlife.org/stationfinder**.

Free Teaching
The daily program, and Truth For Life's entire teaching library of over 3,000 Bible-teaching messages, can be accessed for free online at **truthforlife.org** and through Truth For Life's mobile app, which can be download for free from your app store.

At-Cost Resources
Books and audio studies from Alistair Begg are available for purchase at cost, with no markup. Visit **truthforlife.org/store**.

Where to Begin?
If you're new to Truth For Life and would like to know where to begin listening and learning, find starting point suggestions at **truthforlife.org/firststep**. For a full list of ways to connect with Truth For Life, visit **truthforlife.org/subscribe**.

Contact Truth For Life
P.O. Box 398000 Cleveland, Ohio 44139
phone 1 (888) 588-7884   **email** letters@truthforlife.org
truthforlife.org

"This book took hold of me in chapter one and tightened its grip until, by the end, I was compelled to take up the challenge to 'Dream Small'. I invite you to join me."

ALISTAIR BEGG, Senior Pastor, Parkside Church, Cleveland; Bible Teacher, Truth for Life

"Fresh, invigorating, and liberating. May it be a blessing to all of us ensnared in idolatry of the big."

CHRISTOPHER ASH, Writer-in-Residence, Tyndale House, Cambridge; Author, *Zeal without Burnout*

"*Dream Small* is a needed antidote for our age. Seth Lewis re-centers us, reminding us that the great life is the faithful life. Reading this book was like spending an afternoon with a kind friend who brings you back to what's good, beautiful, and true. I love Lewis's writing style and stories and, most of all, his exhortation to be faithful in the small things, to love God and to love neighbor, to find freedom in dreaming small. If you have ever wondered, *Am I getting this life right?*, this book is for you."

JEN OSHMAN, Author, *Enough About Me, Cultural Counterfeits*, and *Welcome*

"Humble, wise, insightful, and deeply personal, *Dream Small* is an excellent guide to the complex questions of life, giving sound answers grounded in the gospel."

J. MICHAEL THIGPEN, PhD, Provost, Executive President, Pheonix Seminary, Arizona

"This little book by Seth Lewis is a powerful reminder of their importance and a needed call to value supremely what ultimately matters to the God who made us and gives us every ounce of strength. In some ways, it is an easy read. But if we listen to what the Spirit is saying through this book, it is tough, for it demands being counter-cultural, even within the church."

MICHAEL A.G. HAYKIN, Chair, Professor of Church History, Director of The Andrew Fuller Center for Baptist Studies, The Southern Baptist Theological Seminary; Author, *Loving God and Neighbor* with Samuel Pearce

"*Dream Small* is a quiet little volume brimming with overlooked greatness that peels back for us the delights of being an underwhelming collaborator with the true hero, who, in the field of his epic tale, has hidden for you to find, as Seth writes it, 'the mustard seed kingdom that grows in the ordinary things of ordinary life.'"

SOTERIA THOMPSON, Visual Artist, Cross-cultural Worker, Draw From The Heart Art Studio, Phnom Penh, Cambodia

"There is a deep and lasting satisfaction in seeing our dreams come true if, and only if, they are Christ's dreams for us. *Dream Small* gives us the opportunity to realign our life and hopes towards the goals that God has for us rather than those our ego, upbringing or culture thrust on us."

JOHN HINDLEY, Author, *Serving without Sinking, Refreshed*

"*Dream Small* isn't an injunction to begrudgingly 'settle' but to pursue those things that bring lasting joy and ultimately glorify God. If contentment eludes you, let this small book encourage you to evaluate and refocus."

DUSTIN BENGE, Associate Professor of Biblical Spirituality and Historical Theology, The Southern Baptist Theological Seminary; Author, *The Loveliest Place: The Beauty and Glory of the Church*

"In an age of the cult of the big and spectacular, this book summons the reader to a radical reversal of common values. In a doctrinally imaginative and biblically-rooted way, Seth Lewis argues compellingly for a reassessment of dreams, priorities, and perceptions. This is a great book to give to anyone thinking about the meaning of life and what it truly means to be a disciple of Jesus Christ."

EDWIN EWART, Principal, Irish Baptist College

"Seth has written a very helpful meditation on the nature of true success, as defined in the Bible. I finished his book more excited about the value of small daily acts of mundane faithfulness and more wary of the tyranny of striving to achieve non-biblical dreams."

MATT FULLER, Senior Minister, Christ Church Mayfair, London; Author, *Be True to Yourself*

DREAM
SMALL

The Secret Power of the
Ordinary Christian Life

SETH LEWIS

thegoodbook
COMPANY

To my grandfather, Robert Peach, who planted the seed for a book in a surprised college student when he wrote my ideas out as chapter headings on a restaurant serviette.

And to my wife, Jessica, who watered and weeded what grew from that seed, and made it bloom in ways I hadn't imagined. I love you!

Dream Small
© 2022 Seth Lewis

Published by:
The Good Book Company

thegoodbook.com | thegoodbook.co.uk
thegoodbook.com.au | thegoodbook.co.nz | thegoodbook.co.in

ISBN: 9781784987725 | Printed in India

Design by Drew McCall

CONTENTS

BIGGER AND BETTER

"Don't forget the children," she said. "They're worth a lot in the final count."

"I won't, but I don't think they'll be enough. You had a better career, so your net worth will be higher. In the end, that's what matters in The Game Of Life."

I don't usually win The Game Of Life. When we have a board-game night at our house I never get the movie star career card with the big salary, and when I cash in my pink and blue pegs at the end they don't make up for the difference. In the end, it's all about the money.

Let's be fair to Hasbro—they had to have some way to determine a winner in their life-simulation board game. They chose money, which means that everything in the game eventually converts to a currency value—even the children. The player who retires with the most cash value wins. It's a fun game. And there's a logic to it that makes sense to us, because a lot of folks play real life by the same rules.

We've got to live for something, after all. We're here on Earth with time and energy and we need to do something with it, hopefully something that will count, somehow. Hopefully something that will satisfy us, and give us confidence that life is worth living, and the things we're doing are worth doing. Like Hasbro's Game Of Life, we need a goal to reach for, a dream to direct our energy and ambition towards. The trouble is that the rules of real life seem a lot more subjective than the game. We're often encouraged to make our own dreams, and make them as big as possible, but then how do we measure the value of a child against the value of a successful career? How do we measure the value of a close friendship against the value of 1,000 followers on social media? What counts for the most, in the end? Can someone please pass the rule book so I can double check the values and know what I'm supposed to be doing here?

Because whatever the rule book is, I'm not sure I'm following it very well. It seems like any way you measure success, I'm behind. Let me introduce myself.

I am nobody. At least, nobody you've ever heard of, which means almost the same thing, these days. But I've probably never heard of you, either, so we have something in common. And it really is quite common, isn't it? The extraordinary people in the world stand out from the rest of us because of the *extra*, not because of the *ordinary*. The ordinary is just what everybody has. And boy, have I got it. I've got no fabulous wealth or outstanding achievements attached to my name, but I've got so much ordinary you could still call me "extra-ordinary"—not because I have something extra beyond ordinary, just because I've got so much ordinary.

I have scientific proof: I took a workplace assessment once to determine my strengths and weaknesses and find better ways to integrate them with the strengths and weaknesses of my teammates. When the results came back, there was one thing that stood out about my strengths, and that was that nothing stood out. There were a number of areas where I scored well enough, but nothing I was particularly good at, though I know myself there are definitely things I'm particularly bad at. The assessor hastened to reassure me that this can be an advantage. I'm a good all-rounder, passably good at a lot of things, even if I'm not excellent at anything. That's fine, and I see his point, but in that case I'd at least like to be an excellent all-rounder. Like the best all-rounder around, you know, if I can.

Never mind. I can already think of better all-rounders who have more gifts and more highly developed abilities in more areas than I do. The fact is, I'm ordinary. Extra-ordinary. This feels like a confession, an admission of failure. The only people who consistently try to prove that they are ordinary are some high-powered politicians. But then the chauffeur opens the car door for them and they smile, because they know it's just a game and we all know how much power and wealth they really have. Outside of politics, the opposite happens: people work long and hard to convince each other that they have power and wealth, or maybe fame, or talent, or anything at all just as long as it isn't ordinary.

IS GREATNESS THE GREATEST GOAL?

We're not supposed to be ordinary. Or at least, not to admit it. Not to want it, or be satisfied with it. We're supposed to dream big, aim high, and never settle for less. Ordinary is just a stepping stone on the path to greatness, something small and slightly shameful to point back to when we finally do make it big and then we can say to everyone, "Just look how far I've come" and their eyes will grow wide with respect for our strength and determination. They'll think we're great, and if everyone thinks we're great, then we really are, right? In our democratic world, isn't that how greatness works? It makes sense. It also makes sense that greatness is the greatest goal we could go for—I mean, what could be greater than greatness?

That's a good question, actually, because greatness doesn't always seem to end up being all that great. I remember visiting a friend who was retiring after a highly successful career. By any measure I could think of, he had done well. He was well known in his field, and his opinions were well respected wherever he went. While not fabulously wealthy, his family was well-off compared to most. As he showed me around his expensive home, he said, "All of my colleagues have bigger houses. I feel cramped here, but I'm looking at getting something bigger soon". I said nothing, because what could I say? His small house was almost three times the size of mine.

The thing is, he didn't seem three times as happy in his big cramped house. He spent most of our visit complaining about various things and various people. But I remember the old woman who lived in an ancient little shack at the end of our country lane when I was small, and I remember that she was genuinely happy. The light shone through the cracks in her walls, and it shone through the laugh that cracked her face into the kind of deep lines that can only be earned through decades of smiling.

Her house really was cramped, especially when she filled every flat surface with pictures of her many children and grandchildren and great grandchildren. I can't even remember her name now, but I still remember her smile— and the bowl of sweets that was always stocked for visitors. She was not well known, well-off, or even all that well, but she was always welcoming and I wonder: how was this stooped old woman in a shack with no credentials smiling like a winner, while the younger, healthier, richer, far more successful man in the big house was only complaining about his losses? By any measure, her life was smaller. But she found more joy in it than the man who had far surpassed her on the world's ladder of greatness.

How does this happen, and happen so often? I thought the biggest dreams were supposed to bring the biggest happiness and satisfaction and purpose to our lives, so why do I see so many big dreamers so far ahead of me who are still so dissatisfied, even depressed?

Is it possible that bigger is not always better, that more is not always merrier? It is.

Is it possible that dreams can come in more sizes than just big, bigger, and biggest? It is.

Bigger dreams are not what we need. We need better dreams.

BETTER THAN BIGGER

My friend Nancy has found what the better dream is, but you've never heard of her, because her life is small. Her dreams are small, too. Her focus has always been on the people around her, people you've never heard of—like her children, her church, her community, and extra-ordinary people like me. For most of her life she didn't have a big house or even a shack of her own—she raised her daughters in one rented place or another with her husband, Ernie, and they never had much of a financial margin. When my wife and I moved across an ocean to settle in Ireland she barely knew us, but that didn't stop her from welcoming us and feeding us and talking and listening to us like we were her own family. The cups of tea and chats around her table helped us find our feet in a new place, and made us feel unique and special. She even gave us a key to her front door. Later, we realised that we were not alone—we've met people all over Ireland who have had those keys and who feel like they are part of Nancy's family; people who have soaked in the warm hospitality of her table and company and her loving, Scripture-saturated encouragement in the various houses that didn't belong to her.

I'd rather visit Nancy's house than any mansion I can think of. Being part of her wide family circle has been better than any inner circle of influence I've been given access to. Nancy's dreams look small on the normal scales of human greatness, but they have tapped into great reservoirs of joy and love and fullness that have overflowed into the lives of so many ordinary people like me.

I'm not saying that every small life is better and happier than every big, successful life. I've seen small, ordinary people eaten up from the inside out with bitterness over the failure of their big dreams, and I know big achievers who have discovered dreams that are better than their achievements. What I'm saying is that at the end of the day, I'd rather have what Nancy has than any amount of money, or fame, or power. I'm not interested in aiming my dreams at empty promises, no matter how big they look. I want to spend my strength and my short time on this planet on things that really matter, no matter how small they look.

AIMING OUR AMBITIONS

In his first letter to the church in Thessalonica, the apostle Paul writes some instructions on how to live. He speaks about self-control and obedience to God, and emphasises growing in love for others. His last piece of "how to" advice for living is this:

"Make it your ambition to lead a quiet life: You should mind your own business and work with your hands, just as we told you." (1 Thessalonians 4:11)

Ambition. A quiet life.

These two things look like antonyms in a world where dreams are only ever allowed to be big. When I think of ambition, I immediately picture the people who accomplish big things, build big platforms, and end up with big voices that they can use to express themselves in big ways. A "quiet life" is what they left behind, not what they aimed for. And yet somehow Paul puts the two together and apparently he's not telling a joke. He actually thinks that a quiet life of hard work, self-control, obedience to God, and love for others is worthy of aiming our ambitions at (1 Thessalonians 4:1-12). It doesn't even have to be noticed by anyone else.

To say something like this, Paul must have had a very different way of seeing the world than we are used to. He must have had a very different way of measuring value, of determining what is significant, and what a life is for. His own life was big in many ways (which is why we still talk about him and quote him), but the way he lived it shows us how even a big life can be aimed at the same small dreams he told us to pursue. We'll look at this more closely in chapter 7, but for now it's important to note that his advice to others was not to imitate his wide influence or effective strategies or any other metric of worldly success, but rather to focus our lives primarily on smaller things that he says matter most. He even tells us to be ambitious about them. He just wants to make sure that we aim the drive and power of our ambitions in the direction of things that matter much more, and for much longer, than mere fame, fortune or power.

The world around you will constantly encourage you to follow your dreams. That's not bad advice as far as it goes, but I'm asking you to pause first, and take the time to ask an important question that often gets overlooked: just where, exactly, are your dreams leading you? Before you follow your dreams, you need to aim them. And what will you aim them at? The default assumption which says that bigger dreams will always turn out better is simply not true. Where will you find better dreams?

That's what this book is about. I want to show you that there really are better dreams, and encourage you that you can find them right now, right in front of you, right where you are. In the next chapter, we'll see that the whole world is small, including every big dream and every big dreamer in it. Then in chapters 3 and 4, we'll look at where tiny people like us can find real value and real significance. In chapters 5 and 6 we'll flip the normal ladders of success over and point them at what matters most; then in chapter 7 we'll see how every rung on those ladders can be focused on the kind of dreams God made us for. Finally, in chapters 8 and 9, we'll take a closer look at the hard work involved in dreaming small, as well as the rewards—both now and in the future.

So come with me. Our next stop is outer space.

IT'S A SMALL WORLD
AFTER ALL

The camera on the longest selfie stick in the history of humanity was four billion miles away from home when it took a picture of us. The photo is now famously known as "the pale blue dot", because it happened to catch our planet as a point of brightness floating in a ray of sunlight. Astronomer Carl Sagan had suggested that NASA take the picture with their Voyager I probe, and he eloquently described the result:

> *"Look again at that dot. That's here. That's home. That's us. On it everyone you love, everyone you know, everyone you ever heard of, every human being who ever was, lived out their lives. The aggregate of our joy and suffering, thousands of confident religions, ideologies, and economic doctrines, every hunter and forager, every hero and coward, every creator and destroyer of civilisation, every king and peasant, every young couple in love, every mother and father, hopeful child, inventor and explorer,*

every teacher of morals, every corrupt politician, every 'superstar', every 'supreme leader', every saint and sinner in the history of our species lived there on a mote of dust suspended in a sunbeam."

Small.

The more we learn about the universe we live in, the more we see how completely that one word describes us. We are small, all of us, individually and put together, with all our empires and space programmes and skyscrapers. And our dreams? Also small. The biggest dream humans have ever had was to reach the stars. It took many generations of discoveries and accumulated knowledge to get to the point that we could actually do it, and now that we have, our deep space probe promptly turned around and gifted us a glimpse of just how insignificant our planet is in the wider expanse of the universe. Our biggest dream revealed how small we really are, and in the process, made every other "big" dream look microscopic. What else could they be, when we live on a "mote of dust suspended in a sunbeam"?

From the perspective of Voyager I, the pinnacles of human achievement are too small to see—and four billion miles is not even that far in a universe the size of ours. When Voyager I has covered that same distance more than 1,400 times, it will still only be one light-year away from home. It will have to travel a lot farther to reach the edge of the Milky Way, which spans somewhere between 100,000 and 150,000 light-years. And the Milky

Way is just one of more than a hundred billion galaxies—that we know of.

In a universe this size, the tops of our ladders of success don't look so high. Our biggest accomplishments and celebrities are only big by comparison to other tiny things and people. The measuring tape for human greatness is still only measuring centimetres in a universe of light-years. We do love the centimetres, though. I do, anyway. I love to be able to claim, or at least think quietly to myself, that the measure of my life has gone slightly beyond the average. I bet you do, too.

HOW TO MEASURE GREATNESS (IN CENTIMETRES)

To measure anything on our own scale, we have to zoom in to our own little corner on our own little mote of dust at our own little time in history, leaving behind the context of the universe and the long expanse of history that has come before us. If I, for example, want to make myself look greater than you (I've been known to do such things), it will help me to use a frame for my vision that is small enough to make reality appear as a portrait of me, with myself focused perfectly in the centre. If you're looking for yourself, you'd better look on the edges, with the other blurry faces off in the distance. This frame suits me well. If I ever enlarge the frame—or worse, remove it—I fear that my little face will be lost in the overwhelming landscape that is the fullness of true reality. I may not always like the way my face looks, but that doesn't mean I want it to be lost. Nobody wants to be lost. Nobody wants to be just one more in a long line of insignificant specks living out their tiny dreams on "a mote of dust suspended in a sunbeam". Nobody wants to be *that* small. But here I am. Here we all are. And if that's the way it is, maybe I can at least prove that I'm a little less small than the specks beside me. A little less small than you. If all my dreams and ambitions are doomed to be infinitesimal by the objective standards of reality, perhaps they can at least be bigger than yours.

Not to brag, but I'm pretty good at this comparison game. Do you play it, too? You probably do. The question is: What do you base your comparisons on? What measuring sticks are your favourite? You might not have considered this, but you should. It's always best to know what games your mind is playing. But since we're both comparing, I might as well warn you that I might be better than you at thinking I'm better than you. If you give me time I might be able to prove it. With years of practice, I've developed sophisticated ways of showing how my own greatness stretches a little further than most other people's greatness. In order for this to work, though, there is one non-negotiable ground rule: I need to be able to choose the terms. It won't be a beauty contest. Or a race. Or a lot of other things. Have a little patience, while I work to find your weaknesses, so that I can measure my strengths against them. I'm good at measuring. I can make even tiny advantages look devastatingly large. I wonder what tricks you use.

HOW TO LIE WITH THE TRUTH

One of the most useful books I've ever read was an old copy of *How To Lie With Statistics* that I found on my grandfather's bookshelf. I'm not saying that my grandfather was a liar, but only that his book opened my eyes to a world of intrigue which, as it happens, is the world we live in. The overall point was that you don't actually have to change the data to change how the data is perceived. You can get the same effect by simple adjustments to how the data is displayed. One of the most commonly used methods for this is to simply remove the wider context. For example, if you just chop the bottoms off of graphs and remove all the uninteresting sameness, then even small differences in the data can suddenly appear to be hugely significant. Since reading my grandfather's book, I've noticed that this particular method is used constantly in charts about everything from cheese-production levels to rates of unemployment. It goes something like this:

Chart 1: Cheese-Production Levels (This chart is fabricated out of thin air for the purposes of demonstration only. Hopefully it will demonstrate more than my own preoccupation with cheese.)

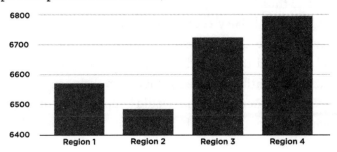

The differences look significant, don't they? But notice that the chart begins with 6,400 units, not 0. In other words, the chart is zoomed in to where the action is. What would it look like if we started from 0 instead?

Chart 2: Cheese-Production Levels, with 0 baseline

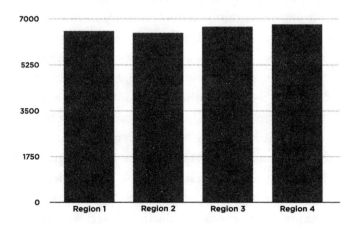

All of a sudden, the differences look a lot smaller. Our perception changes dramatically, even though the data is exactly the same. All we've done is add a bit of context. I say "a bit" of context, because we could go further. Let's say that these cheese-production levels are the output of small regional dairy cooperatives in rural Ireland. If we only compare their numbers against themselves, we'll probably hold the view that producing more than 7,000 units in a month would be a great accomplishment. Maybe it would, for them. But what would happen if we compared their numbers to the global output of all cheese-making dairies in the world? The new chart, with global context, might look more like this:

Chart 3: Cheese-Production Levels, with the context of global output

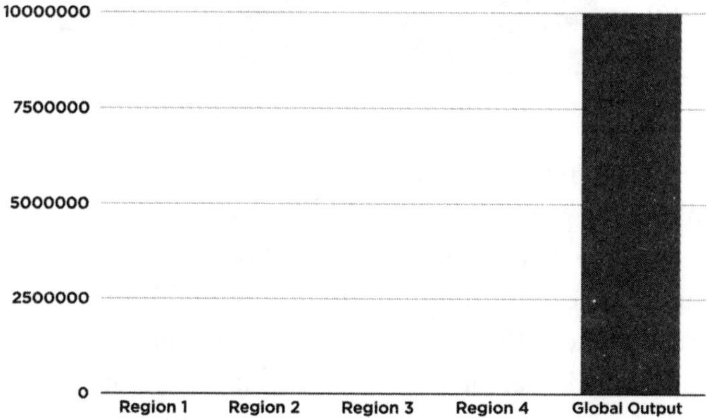

The numbers on the chart for the regional dairy cooperatives are unchanged, yet with the added context of global data, they become too small to even see. The differences that seemed so significant in Chart 1 are now invisible. Now—what would happen if we applied the same methods of measurement to human greatness?

Chart 4: Human-Greatness Aggregate (I don't know how this number is calculated, because everyone has a different formula for it. This can be an advantage, though, because it means that I can use my own personal formula, which happens to emphasise the greatness of the strengths I already possess. Isn't that handy?)

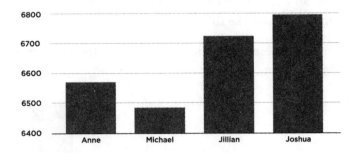

On this chart, it looks like Joshua is the big man in town. Michael is probably ashamed of himself, and Anne can't bear to see Jillian come around and flaunt her successes. But just like the cheese chart, this chart is missing context, making the differences between these four individuals appear to be larger than they actually are. For a more complete picture, we need to start the chart from zero and take into account all that these four individuals have in common—which is a lot. They are all human. They all think, love, work, try and dream. They all learn from their experiences and develop the skills their situations require and they all get tired and have good days and bad days. They all have life and breath and 24 hours in every day. When we start the chart from zero, the differences between these people look a lot smaller.

Chart 5: Human-Greatness Aggregate, with 0 baseline

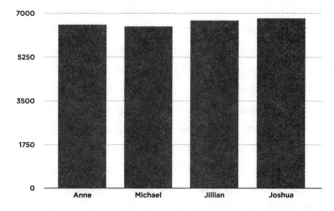

The added context helps us see that the differences people love to obsess over are not as significant as the humanity we all have in common. But this chart is still only focused on four individual humans, and the variations in their levels of greatness are still noticeable. Let's zoom out a bit more, and add in the wider context of the rest of humanity:

Chart 6: Human-Greatness Aggregate, measured against all humans, ever

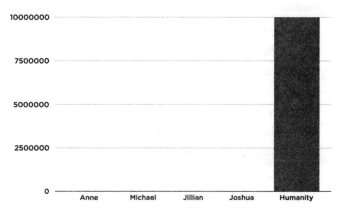

Who's the big man, now? It's impossible to tell, even though the data is exactly the same. In the light of all the billions of humans who have ever lived, these four individuals are easy to miss. Their greatness doesn't even register. Of course there may be a few people who would register on a chart like this—people like Alexander the Great and Genghis Khan and Moses—but that kind of greatness is very rare. And remember: we're still only measuring humans and humanity. If we step out further to Voyager I's perspective, the entire chart of human greatness looks like nothing but a dust speck, which is not very great. Who cares about one bit of dust out of the entire universe? Who cares if one speck on that piece of dust happens to think of itself more highly than the other specks?

THE INSIGNIFICANCE OF SPECKS

I'll be honest—I do care about my own greatness. I care very much about this little planet, and my own short appearance on it. I care about my little life; I still want it to mean something. I still dream of somehow gaining significance beyond my size. Even if it doesn't make sense for me to care, I care about it anyway, and I can't stop. I think you care, too. We all care, which is probably why big dreams are so appealing to us. We want to show how valuable we are, so we work hard to surround ourselves with things that the people around us value. We want to prove that our lives are significant, so we pursue wide recognition and long-lasting legacies. We measure ourselves against each other and climb the ladders of success to the stars, hoping, somehow, to reach beyond the dust we live on.

Are you spending your short time on Earth measuring your own relative greatness against the greatness of other tiny humans? Are you relying on your big dreams to grant you the value and meaning you long for? If so, you're not alone. Even Sagan, after showing us how tiny we are, goes on to tell us that our response should be to dream big for ourselves:

> "The significance of our lives and our fragile planet is then determined only by our own wisdom and courage. We are the custodians of life's meaning ... If we crave some cosmic purpose, then let us find ourselves a worthy goal."

This sounds inspiring, because it offers us a path to the meaning and value we long for. But one persistent question remains: what possible significance and worthy goals can be achieved by the inhabitants of a speck of dust? If it really is up to tiny little us to create our own meaning, then we're in trouble. Sagan really should have been more honest about this. He should have told us plainly that nothing we do actually matters. After shooting our significance in the heart, he might have at least acknowledged the death with a decent burial instead of trying to do CPR and tell us there's still hope. We're too small. We can't deny it. No matter how we present it, the data remains the same. No matter how hard we try, we can't create meaning for ourselves that is big enough to break through our dusty insignificance. Our ladders of success are too short. Our comparison games don't work, either—specks of dust can't make themselves great just by using smaller rulers. We need to face the truth: we can't dream anything big enough to put us on the map. As soon as we look up, our hope for value and meaning shrivels into despair.

Or does it?

THE SIGNIFICANCE OF SPECKS

Have you looked up at the stars on a clear night? It is overwhelming, isn't it? Suddenly, surprisingly, you are small. Your world is small. Your dreams are small. Your problems are small. Your life is small. It doesn't matter how you measure it, or how tiny the person next to you is. You're still small.

Thousands of years ago, a great king looked up and saw the same stars. Suddenly, surprisingly, he was small. His crown was small. His kingdom was small. The little King David asked the question that came obviously to his mind—and he asked it in poetry, because poetry is the language of the overwhelmed:

"*When I consider your heavens,*
the work of your fingers,
the moon and the stars,
which you have set in place,
what is mankind that you are mindful of them,
human beings that you care for them?" (Psalm 8:3-4)

What is mankind? Voyager I proved scientifically that we are a speck of dust in the heavens. When Carl Sagan looked up at those heavens, he saw empty space, devoid of any purpose or meaning beyond what we could build for ourselves. When King David saw the same expanse, he saw the creative work of someone who had set each star in place. Instead of a meaningless void, he saw the careful work of a Creator, to whom the heavens belonged. He saw a God who—amazingly—was mindful of the little lives happening on one small speck in the corner of the Milky Way. David saw a Creator who cared for him, and for the rest of humanity as well.

Having a Creator who cares about us explains a lot. It explains why we can't seem to cure ourselves of the habit of caring about ourselves and the people around us. It explains why we feel that the things we do matter, and that our lives have significance beyond themselves. Having a Creator who cares about us means that our lives *do* matter. Our actions *do* have significance. It means that the value and worth we long for are not secured by our size or the greatness of our achievements, but by the decision of our Creator to value us. After David asks why God would care about us, he goes on to recognise that God has already proven his care for us in how he has treated us:

> *"You have made them a little lower than the angels*
> *and crowned them with glory and honour.*
> *You made them rulers*
> *over the works of your hands." (Psalm 8:5-6)*

David looked up and was overawed by how small we are. Then he looked around and saw that in spite of our small size, we have been crowned with love, honour and responsibility by God himself. He saw that his value and significance—and yours—do not come from being able to climb a little higher than others on the ladders of human achievement. They do not come from having bigger dreams, or bigger achievements, or from measuring yourself against other tiny humans and finding some way to come out on top. Are you still trying to find your significance this way? It's time to stop playing these comparison games. It's time to give up the impossible task of creating your own significance. The biggest dreams on Earth can't do that for you. And they don't have to. There are better dreams. But you won't be able to see them unless you look up and let yourself be overwhelmed—not only by your own smallness but by the greatness of your Creator, and his love for you. Like David, you can turn your eyes up and let your overwhelmed heart overflow in worship. As hard as it may be for us to understand why the God of the universe would care about tiny humans, the God of the universe has shown by his actions that he does, in fact, care about tiny humans. We are small, yes. Very small.

But we are loved.

SIZE MATTERS NOT

I once willingly traded a significant amount of money to buy my wife a string of shiny pearls that took years to form around irritating specks of sand and debris in the mouths of molluscs. I could have saved a lot of that money by buying her some pretty glass beads that were made in a factory, but I didn't. The pearls were harder to get, and that makes them more special. The rock on her ring finger is even smaller, but it's also shinier, and it cost as much as my first car. Here on Earth, it's often the small, shiny, rare things that become the most highly valued of all.

People, on the other hand, are common, and not particularly shiny (although being bald, I'm shinier than most). Have you seen how many of us there are? There's no need to dig or dive to find each other. Sometimes I feel more like digging or diving just to get away from all the crowds of people like me. There's too many of them. In fact, if you can show me a way to get what I want without having to deal with so many of them, I'll pay extra.

This is how my value system works: I am happy to pay a premium to get a string of mollusc mouth spheres, yet also happy to pay a premium to get away from too many people. I automatically assume value for certain rare, shiny dead things, and easily overlook the crowds of living people around me.

It's not just me. This is how the whole world works. This is why diamonds are so expensive, and the lives of diamond miners are cheap. This is why banks are more secure than schools, and why problems like sweatshops and slavery and slums have never been solved. We're so used to measuring value this way that it can be easy to assume that God uses the same kind of measuring systems we do. It's easy to think that God must be just as annoyed by the crowds as we are, and that small, ordinary people (like us) could never mean anything to someone as great and lofty as he is. Indeed, if God himself, sitting on the throne of the universe, used the same measuring systems for value that we've developed down here, then he would have no reason to care about us at all. Do you quietly fear that you are too small and too ordinary to be loved by God? There's good news— it's not true. When God measures our value, he doesn't borrow our measuring tape. He's been very clear on that point. The one who commanded the universe to exist places a particular value on one part of his creation especially. It is not gold, or diamonds, or any other rare, shiny object. It is people. It is us.

Jesus said, "Are not two sparrows sold for a penny? Yet not one of them will fall to the ground outside your Father's care. And even the very hairs of your head are all numbered. So don't be afraid; you are worth more than many sparrows" (Matthew 10:29-31).

God cares about sparrows, but he values people more. After he spoke the universe into existence, he said, "Let us make mankind in our image". In obedience to his command, the dust of the earth became a living, breathing reflection of him. Like any great work of art, God put so much of himself into his creation that by looking at his first humans he could see a reflection of his own heart. He had made something profoundly beautiful that he loved, and he had named us. He had carefully crafted his living masterpiece—out of the dust of the earth.

So Sagan was right, in one sense: we are dust. It is true that Adam and Eve were not big compared to God. It is true, in fact, that they were tiny. But that was no reason for God to love them less. The Mona Lisa is not a big painting, but in our eyes it is priceless. These people were God's magnum opus, as tiny as they were, and he gave them responsibility as rulers over all that he had made, as king and queen under no other authority except himself alone. They were little, but they were loved. They were tiny, but they were brimming with the life that God himself had breathed into them. They were small, but they were given a huge responsibility to rule the world on behalf of the one who had made them.

MADE TO WALK WITH GOD

For a time, everything was right. Adam and Eve ruled creation, and their star-speaking Creator stepped down to talk with them and walk in the garden. Their small size was no barrier to them enjoying close fellowship with the infinite God of everything. We're told that he came and walked in the garden, and that his people spoke to him with familiarity. Like a father asking his children what they will call their new pets, he waited with pleasure to hear them invent names for the animals he had created.

As a father myself, I understand this pleasure. I also wonder what God thought of the names that were chosen. My daughter once named a new stuffed cat "Tesco Black and White" because, well, it was black and white and we bought it at Tesco. I never would have chosen that as a name for anything, but I love it. I love it because I love my daughter, and I love how the name was an expression of her own innocent thought process. I love giving my children good things, and I love watching them take ownership and begin to care for my gifts as their own. I think it's safe to say that God enjoys this, too. He loves to see you delight in his creation, and care for it like he does. He enjoys it when you enjoy a walk in one of his forests, or the cool refreshment of one of his watermelons, or when you accept any of his good gifts as being from his hand. He loves it when you discover the joy of cultivating those gifts and he loves it when you learn to love his creation like he does.

Adam and Eve walked with God, and together they enjoyed the garden he planted for them. Can you imagine being able to ask the artist himself why he made roses smell that way, or what he was thinking of when he put together the duck-billed platypus? Did they ask his advice on the best place to start a new crop of strawberries? Did God give them any hints about what cacao and coffee beans could actually do? I don't know. But I do know that these two tiny humans, who were given responsibility over a universe larger than they could comprehend, felt no shame in speaking freely with God, who made himself available and accessible to them in the garden he gave them. This fact alone teaches us all we need to know about how God sees the relationship between our size and our value.

You, too, are small. But you, too, are made to know God. You are made to relate to him, to experience his love and care, and to express the same to the rest of his creation. Even today, right now, you can speak with the God who spoke the stars into existence. You can talk to him directly about the mundane stuff of daily life, like thanking him that the roses smell how they do, and coffee tastes as good as it does. You can ask for his help with the drama at work, or the family member making bad decisions, or the friend who is suffering in sickness. You can listen to what he says about the role he has for you in the world he made, and seek his strength to live it out. You may be small, but the God of the entire universe loves you and sees you as valuable and significant. You are not too small for him. You are not too ordinary for him. He made you to know him, and he wants you to know him. You may be small, but the High King of everything would like to take a walk with you.

WALKING AWAY

When it comes to God's love, our size is not a problem. Adam and Eve were small, but they enjoyed a perfect relationship with their Maker. It was an untested perfection, though. It was an unforced perfection, because along with all his good gifts of provision and love and authority, God also gave Adam and Eve a choice: they could reject his love, and his gifts, if they wanted to.

God planted a tree, and named it the tree of the knowledge of good and evil. He warned them clearly, saying: "When you eat from it you will surely die" (Genesis 2:17). But when they did choose to eat from it, they found that the fruit was "good for food and pleasing to the eye" (3:6), and no one even got sick. Not immediately, anyway. They both lived long lives after eating, and they had many children. But then they died. And their children died. And we all die, eventually.

The fruit of their action is still killing us. Generation after generation of humans have fallen, filling graveyards and requiring the construction of funeral homes and crematoriums all over the world, all because of the deadly fruit of this seemingly small act of rebellion.

The Bible gives a name to Adam and Eve's appetite for disobedience to their Creator's command: sin. But that name wasn't used when Satan, a fallen angel who had already rebelled against his Maker, tempted Eve to do the same. He made the fruit sound more like power and freedom. He said God was holding out on his people, not allowing them to have the best prize of all, the knowledge of good and evil, which would make them "like God". Never mind that they were already made in God's image, already made with the capacity to reflect his goodness and love and creativity to the world he had given them responsibility over—they dreamed of being "like God" in a different way: completely autonomous and self-sufficient.

What they really wanted, like Satan before them, was to be God. Ever since that day, the human race has carried on in a stubborn refusal to be content with our privileged place in God's universe, and the responsibilities he has entrusted to us. God literally gave us the world, but we wanted his throne.

This is a big dream. Too big. The prophets of old tried to warn God's people that this was a dangerous way for dependent dust motes to speak, but they were not listened to. Long before Carl Sagan, the prophet Isaiah was already using the same language to describe us:

> "Surely the nations are like a drop in a bucket;
>   they are regarded as dust on the scales;
>   he weighs the islands as though they were fine dust."
> (Isaiah 40:15)

Dust on the scales; not even enough to weigh. And that's the nations, not the individuals. We were wrong to assume that God uses the same measuring tools we do. We weren't even close. Yet here we are, the dust that doesn't even begin to move the scales, shouting up and shaking our microscopic fists at our Maker, telling him to move over and make way for our own personal ambitions. It would be too preposterous to believe, if it weren't so terribly true.

To make it even worse, this came after God had already stooped down to our level to plant us a paradise and share with us his authority over it. After lifting us from the dust and the insignificance of our size to the heights of dizzying prominence, our thanks to God for this was to use his own gifts against him. Should we expect to be successful in this war against reality? No.

We're already losing. We have cut ourselves and the world that was given to us away from God, like a branch cut away from the vine, and then we are surprised when everything starts withering. What else could it do? We were never made to have a life of our own; we were made to draw constantly from the never-ending life of God. "When you eat from it, you will certainly die" was a curse, absolutely, but there was no magic in it. It was a statement of fact. If we will not draw life from God, we will not have life at all. There is simply nowhere else to find it. Not that we haven't looked; we've spent the ages of history building and planning and trying and dreaming up every other possibility we can think of, and yet here we are, still withering away slowly, like branches without a vine.

What about you? Where are you looking for life? Are you dreaming that you will find it in romance, or in establishing a family? Are you hoping to discover it in creative expression, or in feeding yourself with non-stop pleasure? Maybe you are trying to build it through your accomplishments, or grow it in your friendships, or find it in your travels? All of these are good gifts from your Creator, but not one of them has the power to give you the life you were made to find in God. Separated from him, every other good gift fades away, eventually, like cut flowers in a vase.

This is humanity: we are small, and we are dying. Our dreams of finding life and value and meaning somewhere besides God have failed, every time, and are failing, still. As we move ourselves and our world away from God, we are like the embers flying up from a campfire—still flickering with the glory we were given, even as we slowly fade away into ashes and dust. Apart from God, the curse comes true: "For dust you are, and to dust you will return". We had significance and importance far beyond our size, and we shone with it. We had an intimate connection to infinite life, and we severed it. We had paradise, and we tossed it aside in a blind attempt to rob more from the one who gave it to us. The barrier between humanity and God was not caused by the difference in our size. It was built by our own hands, established through our choice to reject the love of our Creator and our attempt to create our own life without him.

SMALL, SINFUL AND STILL VALUED

Are you afraid that you are too small or too ordinary for God to love? You're not. His love is too big to be put off by your small size. But what about sin? Are you afraid that you are too sinful for God to love? You're not. His love is bigger than that, too. After all we had done against him, God, the giver of all our good gifts, kept giving. He didn't give up on us. It's true that he would have been completely justified to leave us to our own devices. He would have been well within his rights to crush us with justice for our crimes and leave us to die the slow death of those who reject their own source of life. But instead, he gave us a gift even bigger than the world he made for us: he freely chose to make himself small and became one of us—imagine! Jesus, who is God himself, became one more speck of dust on Earth, and he did it on purpose, so that he could carry the weight of human sin on his own human shoulders.

Jesus knew we had no hope of climbing up to him, so he climbed down to us and willingly died the death we deserve. He knew that it was the only way to satisfy his own justice for sin and still be able to bring us back to himself. Back to life. Back to everything he made us for. After three days in the grave—what should have been our grave—he rose again, proving once and for all that the life he now offers to dying humans is more powerful than death itself. In our sin, we tried to make ourselves as big as God, and all we won for ourselves was death. In his love, God made himself as small as we are, and he won his children life.

Why would he do this? In the Gospel of John, Jesus tells us plainly that he came to save us because "God so loved the world" (3:16). If we're honest, it's obvious that God does not love humans because we are impressive—we aren't. He does not love people because we are good—we aren't that, either.

The good news for us is that God does not operate the way we do. He does not value the way we do. After all we have done against him, he continues to love and reach out to the people he has made. Of course, we can still refuse him. We can still carry on in our search for life apart from him. In that case, he will honour our choice, and leave us to the consequences. This is, quite literally, hell. But the offer of life is good, and available to anyone, as Jesus says in John 10:10: "I have come that they may have life, and have it to the full". The only requirement he gives us is that we end our foolish rebellion and return to him. His invitation is simple: come, and live.

> "For this is what the high and exalted One says—
>   he who lives for ever, whose name is holy:
> 'I live in a high and holy place,
>   but also with the one who is contrite
>   and lowly in spirit,
> to revive the spirit of the lowly
>   and to revive the heart of the contrite.'" (Isaiah 57:15)

The God who spoke the universe into existence loves to live with the people who come back to him. He forgives, and revives, and restores them. He values them. When Jesus came to Earth to save us from our sin, he also turned our measuring systems upside down and taught us that our value is not what we thought it was, and that it does not come from the places we thought it came from. The good news is that God is not only far bigger than we are in size, power and glory, but also in love, mercy and compassion. The good news is that you don't have to fear that you are too small, too ordinary or too sinful to be loved by God. The good news is that you don't have to try to use your dreams to make yourself big enough or good enough to love, or to somehow create your own value and meaning and life. You can find all of this, and so much more, where it was all along: in the love of your Creator, who also became the Saviour of anyone who will come to him.

Will you come?

When you come to Jesus, everything changes—including your dreams.

A SMALL PART,
A BIG STORY

We are small, but we are loved. Our value is not derived from our actions, dreams or achievements, or by how we collectively measure each other on these things; and yet it is secure—it is built in, breathed in, by our Creator. In this light, the world looks completely different. In this light, your life looks completely different. Suddenly, you are free from the impossible task of dreaming up your own value and meaning. You don't have to prove your worth with your performance in the classroom, or on the job, or in some area of talent. You don't have to create your own significance with dreams that go further and reach higher than the dreams of others. You don't have to dream and work and impress your way to being loved, appreciated, and understood. But where do we go from here? If you're not dreaming of those things, then what are dreams for?

It would be helpful here to think of the world, and our own lives, as stories. This is not just a useful mental image, it's just true—the world really is a story, and so is your life, and so is mine. So the question for me (and you) is, how will I approach the story of my life? There are two basic directions I can go:

1. I can see myself as the author of my own story, and dream up the best plot, action and ending that I can for myself.

Or,

2. I can see myself as a character in a story that is bigger than I am, and align my dreams with a plot that is bigger than my life.

If I look for guidance from popular culture on which of these options to choose, option 1 will be the overwhelming favourite. The advice may take many forms in many mediums, but it will almost always point me towards taking authorship of my own life and pointing my dreams in whatever direction I personally choose for them to go. So Elsa sings to me in her power anthem that there's "no right, no wrong, no rules for me", and Frank Sinatra croons in my ear that "I did it my way", while Oprah Winfrey just tells me directly: "You are the author of your own life".

This feels empowering—at least, it feels that way as long as things are going smoothly, according to my plan. But what happens when the plot twists off in a direction I didn't tell it to go? When I put the work in, but still get passed over? When the person I care about doesn't care about me, or the sickness comes on the one day I needed most to be well? In a moment like that, it's harder to claim authorship for my own life. After all, authors are all-knowing, all-powerful, and are able to guide the story and every event and character towards their desired ending. As much as I'd like to, I can't do those things. I can control my own choices, but I can't control the choices of others, and there's really not a lot I can do about most of the events around me. When reality doesn't align with my plan, it shows me clearly that I am not the author of my life. I'm inside the story, trying to make the best choices I can, without the advantages of omniscience and omnipotence. To put it another way, I'm a character, not an author.

If I ignore this and continue to act like the author of my own story, I'll end up frustrated and angry, and probably depressed. The people around me won't stop going off the scripts I write for them, and the scenes I set for myself won't always look like the scenes I face in reality. Even the things that do end up going to plan often don't bring the lasting good results that I hope for, and in the end, every one of my dreams and ambitions will eventually crumble back into the dust they came from, like sand castles giving way to the oncoming tide.

Thankfully, the significance of my story does *not* have to depend on me doing the best I can to dream up and achieve worthy goals for myself, like Carl Sagan and a thousand celebrities tell me to do. The reality that

God made me in his own image and loved me enough to pay for my sin to bring me back to himself gives me conclusive proof that my story is part of something much bigger than my own private one-volume autobiography, *The Life and Times of a Dust Speck*.

A BIGGER STORY

God is up to something, and it's big. It's much bigger than I am, stretching back to before creation, and forward into never-ending eternity. And yet, it still touches me, in my own little corner of time and space. When I step back to take this in, I might be afraid—can a little life like mine matter in a story that is bigger than the universe and longer than history? The Bible answers with a resounding yes. The little King David, who sang of his amazement at how the God of everything cares for tiny men and women, also sang of this truth:

"For you created my inmost being;
  you knit me together in my mother's womb.
I praise you because I am fearfully and wonderfully made;
  your works are wonderful,
  I know that full well.
My frame was not hidden from you
  when I was made in the secret place,
  when I was woven together in the depths of the earth.
Your eyes saw my unformed body;
  all the days ordained for me were written in your book
  before one of them came to be." (Psalm 139:13-16)

The Maker of galaxies stooped to build my unseen body, and he built it according to his plan. I am not mass-produced; I am not an accident. I am a work of living art, carefully designed by the greatest artist of all time. Every detail of my body was formed according to the specific plan and purpose of God, because he wanted me to be a character in his story. Did you see it? David said that "all the days ordained for me were written in your book before one of them came to be". Pause for a moment and let that sink in—God has a book, and every single day is written in it. God has a story, and he wrote me into it. Every single day. Me doing dishes, me taking walks, me talking with neighbours about the weather and discussing politics and grasping for coffee with bleary eyes in the morning and all of these things, and so many more: these are written by God's hand in God's story.

The book belongs to God; he's the author. This means, of course, that I am not. I am a character, placed in a story that is much bigger than I am. This story is not my autobiography. It does not start with my birth, and it does not end with my death. Still, the author gave me a role in it, a role that no one else can fill. He invented me, specifically, to fill a gap in his plot, because evidently the story of eternity would not be complete without tiny little me. The same is true for you, and it's good news.

It's good news because it means that instead of the constant pressure to create meaning for your life out of thin air, you can discover that you already have a role in something much bigger than yourself, something truly meaningful for all of eternity. It means that instead of driving yourself to create a legacy for your own little name, you can discover that your own little name is already known, already loved, carefully created, and never forgotten by the King of heaven himself. It means that even if the story you're in does not go according to your plan, your meaning and purpose in life cannot be destroyed.

That's a big deal. Where else can you find this kind of security? Money can be lost. Fame can be forgotten. Health and strength can fade to sickness and frailty. If all you have are big dreams for yourself, created out of your own head and for your own purposes, then those dreams are vulnerable and can easily be destroyed by the suffering you face in life. The plot twists that take you away from your plan for your own happy ending and leave it out of your reach also leave the meaning you made for yourself out of your reach.

But it was God who breathed life into you, and he did it for a reason. It's been said before, but history is *his story*, including every detail and every character. The story God is writing is not a library with billions of individual, separate biographies, most of which are already lost and forgotten. It is an epic with billions of characters, yet a unified whole that slowly works its way from the introduction through countless pages of ongoing problems and rising action to a climax and final resolution.

In his story, God writes promises to sinful people, and keeps his promises even when we don't keep ours. He writes warnings and judgment to wake us up, and comfort and joy to draw us in. His story includes nations and kings and widows and orphans, battles and cities and deliverance. As the plot unfolds, we see over and over again that humanity's rebellion is deep and stubborn, and over and over again that God's love is even more so. The climax is the cross and resurrection. The ending is, quite literally, heaven.

FINDING YOUR PLACE IN THE STORY

The same God who is writing all of this has a purpose for you. Your life can be part of the biggest story ever told. Your short time on this planet can contribute to the unfolding epic of redemption and restoration. All you have to do is take up the role he made you for, and stop trying to be the author of your own story.

But that's a lot to ask, isn't it? It's hard to give up the leading role. It's hard to stop trying to write reality to fit your dreams. As impossible as it is to control life, it's also difficult to stop trying. It's hard to hand over control to the real author. It feels like a loss, and it feels that way for a good reason: because it is. It's a loss of control, and it could be a loss of some of the dreams you had for yourself. The role God has for you in his story might not look like the role you were writing for yourself. It might not include some of the good things that you wanted, like the perfect marriage and family, or the high-powered career, or the influencer status. Or maybe it will. I'm not the author of your story, so I don't know.

What I do know is this: no dream (no matter how big) and no gift (no matter how wonderful) can satisfy you and give you the unshakable joy and life you long for when these are separated from the giver. The romance will not cure your selfishness (I'm married to the love of my life—I know). The promotion will not make everyone respect you. It may not even make you respect yourself. The extra income will not solve all of your problems, and it may bring a few new ones with it. None of these dreams are bad, but none of them can compare to the dreams God has for you.

Are you dreaming of great things for yourself? There is nothing greater than knowing God and experiencing his love. Are you working to build a legacy that will outlast you? Nothing can outlast God's kingdom. Do you want people to know your name? Your Creator already does. Do you want to gain access to the inner circles of power and influence? The children of the King of kings are always welcome in his throne room (Hebrews 4:16). Do you want your life to make a difference in the world? God has a unique place for you in the greatest rescue story ever told.

Jesus describes his people as his bride, his body on Earth, the ambassadors of his kingdom, and the temple of God. We are growing and bearing his fruit from the seeds of his new life that he planted in us. We are a city on a hill and a lamp on a stand, shining with his light, loving with his love, living in the power of his undying life. Every moment of every day for every citizen of God's kingdom becomes alive with eternal significance, becomes an opportunity to display the never-ending kingdom of God in time and space, and by doing so, to send shock waves into eternity.

DOORKEEPERS AND KINGS

Imagine! Tiny little me, and tiny little you, being given roles like this in the "Epic of the Ages". Will other people measure them as big roles? Will they ignore them as small ones? Who cares! You have a part to play in the greatest story ever told, a part specially designed for you by the author himself. The smallest of roles in his story is better, and far more significant, than the lead role in your own. Here's what the little king of Israel had to say about it:

> "Better is one day in your courts
>   than a thousand elsewhere;
> I would rather be a doorkeeper in the house of my God
>   than dwell in the tents of the wicked." (Psalm 84:10)

Doorkeepers don't get much recognition. There are no Doorkeeper of the Year awards (that I know of), and if there's a red carpet, they are standing beside it, not walking on it. The crowds and photographers walk past them without a glance, as if they were part of the scenery. Kings, on the other hand, get plenty of attention. They live at the top of human society, far above the lowly servants who perform simple tasks like opening doors. Yet here we have a human king whose consuming desire is not to be recognised for the greatness of his work, but only to be sure that he is close to his God as he does it—even if the work is only opening doors.

Opening doors is not impressive. Anyone can do it. In fact everyone does it, every day, including children. That's not the point. The little king saw that the significance of the act was not in how impressive or skilled it was, but in how close he could be to God while doing it. David considers one day of menial work done near to God and in service to him to be more significant than a thousand days away from God serving his own big dreams. He knew that in God's book, doorkeepers who work in fellowship with God, faithfully serving him, are more celebrated than the greatest of human celebrities who refuse to give up trying to take the author's place.

Jesus spoke this way, too. He said, "If anyone gives even a cup of cold water to one of these little ones who is my disciple, truly I tell you, that person will certainly not lose their reward" (Matthew 10:42). He also said, "What good will it be for someone to gain the whole world, yet forfeit their soul?" (16:26). In other words, we can reach the top of every ladder of human success, and still lose it all. Or we can gain an eternal re-ward by giving away a cup of cold water for the sake of God's kingdom. The message is clear: the significance of our actions here and now is not at all determined by the wealth and applause they generate. The significance of our actions here and now is always determined by their connection to God and the story he is writing, the eternal kingdom he is building.

This is freeing. Aligning your dreams with God's story means that you can "seek first his kingdom and his righteousness" (6:33) without having to worry about how well your achievements stack up on the scales of human measurement. You can joyfully and gratefully take your place in God's bigger story and stop living under the constant pressure of trying to be the author of your own. You can be a character, written in for a specific purpose at exactly this time and place in history, and you don't have to know or control every detail to know and be confident that every detail has significance. It means that even if your life does not go to your plan, it can still be part of a bigger, better, and more beautiful plan. It means that you are free to pursue dreams that the world around you overlooks and measures as small, knowing that your Creator sees and rewards even cups of cold water given in his name. You can know that he is using every act of faithful obedience, big and small, to move the plot forward towards a grand finale far better than any dream you could write for yourself.

Your role may be small in the grand sweep of history, but there is a purpose behind it. Your life may be small, but it is part of a big story, a beautiful story of redemption and life, of love and loss and restoration, of happily-ever-after beyond imagination. This is God's story. And if you are his, then this is your story. Are you still trying to write your own? Or are you ready to take your place in the Epic of the Ages?

THE UPSIDE-DOWN
LADDER

The new guy was effortlessly working the room. He told a joke and everyone laughed, and I laughed. He was nice, and I had no reason not to like him except that everyone liked him and they wouldn't like me. I had been in the youth group for years, and the church for as long as I could remember, but when I told a joke they pretended they couldn't hear me. I told it louder and their faces scrunched. I stopped talking and they pretended I didn't exist. Eventually I decided that I would take up less space on the edge of the room, with my eyes down. But there was a problem: the edges were already crowded with eyes looking down, trying not to exist too loudly. At first I was annoyed. Then I saw them.

I had been so focused on the new kid and how he was being welcomed among the Rulers of the High Places that I nearly forgot there was anyone else in the room. But there they were, right in front of me. We were together, a wall of outcasts looking down. But even as our eyes scanned the floor, we were all looking for a way to climb the ladder of acceptance and popularity. We revered the ones who lived above us, we respected them and played by their rules, even as they continually brushed us aside. But that night when I looked around me, something was different: all of a sudden, the rejected people around me didn't look like lowly nobodies anymore, like social negatives who would only bring my own status down the more I interacted with them. All of a sudden, they looked like people. They looked like me.

That night, something inside of me began to shift. I wanted to know these people. I wanted to find out what they were like, and what they were interested in. I wanted to discover why God made them the way he did, and to see them the way he does, instead of assuming the same measuring system as the "Rulers of the Room". I started to see, dimly at first, that the "Rulers" were wrong. God made the people on the edges in his own image, and he loves them. He also loves to populate his eternal kingdom with the kind of people that the "Rulers" overlook, as Paul says in his first letter to the Corinthians:

> *"Brothers and sisters, think of what you were when you were called. Not many of you were wise by human standards; not many were influential; not many were of noble birth. But God chose the foolish things of the world to shame the wise; God chose the weak things of the world to shame the strong. God chose the lowly*

things of this world and the despised things—and the things that are not—to nullify the things that are."
(1 Corinthians 1:26-28)

If the people on the edges are so valuable to God, then I want to know them, too. If these people are so important to him, then I want them to be important to me. That night in youth group, I went into the room looking for the most influential people to talk to, searching for ways to impress the gatekeepers of status, and reaching for the next rung on the ladder up to social prominence. By the time I left, a new goal was beginning to form: I wanted to find the people who felt like I felt that night, and see if I could lift their heads and enjoy their company. I wanted to see everyone in the room—both high and low—as people, loved by their Maker and worthy of my respect and attention.

I realise that this is not the most efficient way to network my way up the ladders of social success. Treating everyone this way can sometimes have the opposite effect, because the "Rulers" have rules about who you ought (and ought not) to associate with. That's fine with me: I see now that the people on the edges are more important than the entire ladder of success. Just look at how Jesus lived.

THE KING WHO CLIMBED DOWN
With all of the power and privilege that he had held in heaven, you might expect that when Jesus came to Earth, he would come to the top of human society. You might expect that his home on Earth would have been the closest

thing to heaven anyone had ever seen, always filled with the most powerful people, tables laid out with the most exquisite food, and wardrobes containing the most stylish clothes. He could have come to us demanding the very best that the world has to offer, and his demands would have been completely legitimate. He made our world. He made us. He gave us life, and gave us the world. If anyone had a right to come and be served, he did. This makes the approach he actually took even more surprising, as we see in the Gospel of John, chapter 13:

> *"Jesus knew that the Father had put all things under his power, and that he had come from God and was returning to God; so he got up from the meal, took off his outer clothing, and wrapped a towel around his waist. After that, he poured water into a basin and began to wash his disciples' feet, drying them with the towel that was wrapped round him ...*

> *"... When he had finished washing their feet, he put on his clothes and returned to his place. 'Do you understand what I have done for you?' he asked them. 'You call me "Teacher" and "Lord", and rightly so, for that is what I am. Now that I, your Lord and Teacher, have washed your feet, you also should wash one another's feet. I have set you an example that you should do as I have done for you. Very truly I tell you, no servant is greater than his master, nor is a messenger greater than the one who sent him. Now that you know these things, you will be blessed if you do them.'" (v 3-5, 12-17)*

The speaker of galaxies, whose superlatives are beyond measuring, who knew very well that he had "all things under his power", made himself small. Even more, he made himself humble. The King of kings "did not come to be served, but to serve" (Matthew 20:28). The one man who had literally every claim to fame, power, authority and privilege used his high position to bend down and wash the smelly feet of a dozen ordinary tradesmen. He even washed between the dirty toes of the man he knew would betray him.

In doing this, Jesus turned all of our ideas about power and privilege, all of our measurements of greatness and glory, on their head. He already had more of the power and fortune that humans fight and die for than we could even imagine. Yet he set it all aside to give himself in service for the most ordinary kind of common people, the kind of people that are overlooked and oppressed by the ones who usually impress us with their greatness. The King of heaven spent the majority of his time on Earth with tax collectors, sinners and uneducated tradespeople. He ignored the established rules for getting ahead, offended the elite gatekeepers of status, and went out of his way for people who couldn't contribute anything to his social advancement—like little children, scandalous women, the marginalised poor, the unpopular rich (like Zacchaeus the tax-collector) and beggars suffering with debilitating sickness.

He hadn't forgotten who he was. He knew exactly where he had come from, and where he was going. Even as he washed the feet of his disciples, we're told first that he "knew that the Father had put all things under his power, and that he had come from God and was returning to God". He knew that his position as the true power of the universe was never under threat, and that he would soon sit again on heaven's throne. What did he do with this knowledge? He washed the dirty feet of tiny, ungrateful humans and went to the cross for their sins. He humbled himself and served, even to the point of death, knowing full well what his service would accomplish.

CLIMBING DOWN IN CONFIDENCE

If I am going to follow Jesus' lead towards serving others, it is important for me to know, like Jesus, where I come from, and where I am going. I am not the Lord of heaven, but I have been made in his image. God himself breathed life into my body, and he did it for a reason. He wrote me into his book. He loved me, and died to bring me back to himself. This is where I come from. And where am I going? As his child, he has promised to bring me with him to his eternal kingdom, a kingdom where God's people experience the never-ending abundance of his generosity. As Psalm 36:8-9 puts it:

> *"They feast on the abundance of your house;*
> *you give them drink from your river of delights.*
> *For with you is the fountain of life;*
> *in your light we see light."*

Jesus gave up all his advantages knowing full well that his identity was secure and his future was glorious. In a similar way, if you and I are confident in who God created us to be and confident of his promises for the future through the work of Christ, then we are secure enough to give ourselves in sacrificial service here and now, no matter how much it may cost us. Yes, it could cost you the respect of the self-appointed gatekeepers of social status. It could mean that people overlook you, because you give your time and attention to people they overlook. It could cost you resources and energy that could have been used for your own personal benefit instead.

Then again, how much more personal benefit do you need when the God of the universe has already gifted you the eternally secure treasures of heaven? How much more status do you need, when your name is known by God and written in his book for ever? Nothing you give in service on Earth can compare with the riches that God has already given his children. If you are his, then you can follow your Saviour in service and share his riches with the people around you, fully confident that you will lose nothing by imitating his generosity. On the contrary— the blessings and rewards that Jesus promises repeatedly to his servants do not go to those who dream the biggest dreams for themselves, but rather to those who love, value, and sacrifice themselves for the small people that our king left heaven to rescue.

CLIMBING DOWN TO GLORY

He came to save small people, because that's the only size people come in. The fact that he came to the lowest and smallest of humanity is stunning, but not as stunning as the fact that he came to humanity in the first place. The biggest step down for Jesus was leaving heaven. After that ' giant leap, the steps between human social classes were tiny. The best of our palaces wouldn't be that impressive to a man who is at home on heaven's throne. Nothing we have on our tiny speck of dust in the stars could compare to where he came from.

From his vantage point, it was easy to see through the pretension of human power and privilege, the lie that somehow collecting piles of rare and beautiful things around us makes us more valuable, the fiction that somehow getting other people to serve us makes us more worthy of being served. When Jesus came, he came all the way down to the bottom rung of humanity's ladder of success. He didn't play the Game of Life by our rules. His journey of humiliation went against our normal assumptions about what power is for and contradicted our normal priorities for what life is about.

No wonder God said in Isaiah that "my thoughts are not your thoughts, neither are your ways my ways" (55:8). He came as Lord, and yet washed dirty feet like the lowest of servants. He took our ladders of success and purposefully flipped them over. Then he said, "Now that you know these things, you will be blessed if you do them" (John 13:17).

You will be blessed if you use the ladders of success to go down in service, instead of up in personal ambition.

You will be blessed if you give yourself to serve others, instead of using others to serve yourself.

You will be blessed if you use your leg up over others as leverage for your arm, reaching down to lift them.

In God's kingdom, "the last will be first, and the first will be last" (Matthew 20:16). In his hierarchy, "the greatest among you will be your servant. For those who exalt themselves will be humbled, and those who humble themselves will be exalted" (23:11-12). Read that again. Can you believe it?

In God's kingdom, greatness is measured in service, and honour is measured in humility. The path up to glory is sloped down. As humanity sweats and climbs and searches the high places for blessing and joy and satisfaction, Jesus tells us that all of these things and more are waiting, right under our feet, in common things like the mud between the toes of fishermen.

This feels backwards. Heaven's hierarchy looks upside down. The reality, though, is that our world is upside down, and God's kingdom is right side up. Jesus' seemingly topsy-turvy way of life was exactly the way we were all intended to live. The reason it looks so strange to us now is because our rebellion against God has led us so far from his good plan for us. We're the ones that tipped the world over, with all of its ladders and dreams. Jesus is the one that sets it right again.

TURNING THE LADDERS AROUND

If you let him reshape your perspective, you'll begin to see the reality that honour in God's kingdom is far more valuable than any amount of human status or influence. You'll begin to recognise the humility of your smallness, and the exaltation of being loved by God and gifted a role in his unfolding epic of history. You'll begin to appreciate the value that God has placed on the humans around you, and you'll stop measuring that value by the greatness of their dreams or successes on Earth. You'll begin to see that every single human you ever meet is specially created to be a living picture of God himself, with an eternal soul that will continue long after the greatest of human accomplishments is forgotten. When you see these things, your priorities change. When you know these things, your dreams change.

Your approach changes, too. Think about what rooms you'll be in this week. Who will be there with you? When you walk in and see them there, what will your goal be? The answer to that question is more important than the room itself, or your position in it. It doesn't matter if it's a boardroom or a classroom or a warehouse or a house party. It could be the gardening club or the Garden City Rugby Club—if there are people, there are ways you could work to impress them. There are things you could do that might get their attention. There are conversations you could have that might increase your status, especially if you can have them with the right people. If you focus your dreams and your energy on your own advancement, you really can get ahead of others. And you can run ahead of God's plans for you, ahead of people he loves, ahead of the joy of giving, and ahead of the honour he gives to those who humble themselves in service like his. "The greatest among you will be your servant." A servant should not enter the room to advance themselves. A servant should enter the room to serve. How will you serve the people in the rooms you spend time in this week?

Jesus promised that those who turn the ladders of success over like he did will find blessings. Some of these blessings are the rewards he promises so generously in his eternal kingdom. Others are experienced now, like the deep friendships that grow so well when you don't base your relationships on mutual social advantage. Or the wonderful freedom of not having to play by the unpredictable rules of advancement politics. Or the confidence that only comes from entering a room not to impress or network or draw attention to yourself, but to serve. When you flip the ladders over, you discover that shared joy is deeper than lonely success; friendship is happier than wealth; and people are more precious than anything on Earth.

The world around us measures greatness in being served, not in serving. They count the ones who are served the most as the most blessed, like comfortable kings and queens who can click their fingers and send people running for their every whim. The King of heaven disagrees. He stepped down from his throne to wash feet like the lowest of servants, and told us that the heights of heaven's glory belongs to the people who climb down in humility, like he did. He says that the greatest blessings are found by those who get their hands dirty in service, like he did. The world sees this way of life as backwards, and measures these dreams as small, but Jesus said: "The greatest among you will be your servant. For those who exalt themselves will be humbled, and those who humble themselves will be exalted". My Saviour won me a place in his eternal kingdom, a kingdom of joyful service, a kingdom completely different from the realms of earthly power and privilege I see around me. My King turned the ladder of success upside down and showed me that the path to the heights leads down. He blazed the trail himself.

"Now that you know these things, you will be blessed if you do them." (John 13:17)

6

SMALL PEOPLE,
BIG VALUE

nner-city Chicago, 1920s: The door opened at the YMCA, a Christian association (that's the "C" and "A") established to provide food, lodging, help, and gospel-fuelled support to young men (that's the "Y" and "M") in need. The man who stepped in was desperate. The man who greeted him was my great-grandfather, Horace Peach.

Horace didn't have to be at the door. He had been offered higher positions in the hierarchy of the YMCA. He could have been in an office making decisions, wielding influence over the organisation, holding a more noticeable title and drawing a more significant salary. He turned them all down. He wanted to stay at the door, because he wanted to be the first one to welcome the hopeless strangers who came in. And for years, and decades, and for countless desperate cases, he did just that. He didn't have a lot for himself—when the Great Depression hit, he lost his house and everything he had put into it. He moved his family and started over and kept on giving himself for others. After he died, someone described him this way: "When he talked to you, you felt important". He really thought you were important, whoever you were, and whatever struggles you were facing. He spent his life serving important people that most of the world overlooked as hopeless strangers.

In Psalm 84, King David said he would rather be a doorkeeper in the house of his God than live in luxury without him. My great-grandfather lived these words out in real life. When he died, his obituary summarised his life with four words: "Friend of the friendless". It was a life lived in imitation of his Saviour, who was known as a friend of "tax collectors and sinners" (Luke 5:30): the kind of people that anyone in good standing would avoid because being close to them would damage their status. Jesus welcomed them; he valued them. So did Horace; and so should we.

God does not appreciate it when we overlook the people he made in his own image and treat them as if they were meaningless or disposable. We should see the role they were created for in God's story, not ours. Every human you see today was planned and crafted carefully for their role in God's story. When he made them, he didn't make a mistake. Every human you see today is invited to come to God and receive forgiveness and a place in his own family. Which means that every human you see today is God's creative masterpiece, and some of them are already God's adopted children.

As a father myself, I can tell you that there are strong feelings involved when I see someone mistreat one of my children. They are not good feelings. On the other hand, when someone treats one of my children well, I take it as a personal favour. It turns out, I'm not alone in this. Jesus was clear that God feels the same way about how we treat his family members:

"When the Son of Man comes in his glory, and all the angels with him, he will sit on his glorious throne. All the nations will be gathered before him, and he will separate the people one from another as a shepherd separates the sheep from the goats. He will put the sheep on his right and the goats on his left.

"Then the King will say to those on his right, 'Come, you who are blessed by my Father; take your inheritance, the kingdom prepared for you since the creation of the world. For I was hungry and you gave me something to eat, I was thirsty and you gave me something to drink, I was a stranger and you invited me in, I needed clothes and you clothed me, I was ill and you looked after me, I was in prison and you came to visit me.'

"Then the righteous will answer him, 'Lord, when did we see you hungry and feed you, or thirsty and give you something to drink? When did we see you a stranger and invite you in, or needing clothes and clothe you? When did we see you ill or in prison and go to visit you?'

"The King will reply, 'Truly I tell you, whatever you did for one of the least of these brothers and sisters of mine, you did for me.'

"Then he will say to those on his left, 'Depart from me, you who are cursed, into the eternal fire prepared for the devil and his angels. For I was hungry and you gave me nothing to eat, I was thirsty and you gave me nothing to drink, I was a stranger and you did not invite me in, I needed clothes and you did not clothe me, I was ill and in prison and you did not look after me.'

"They also will answer, 'Lord, when did we see you hungry or thirsty or a stranger or needing clothes or ill or in prison, and did not help you?'

"He will reply, 'Truly I tell you, whatever you did not do for one of the least of these, you did not do for me.'"
(Matthew 25:31-45)

Jesus is giving us a glimpse at the end of the book, allowing us to read the last page of the story first. I tell my children not to do this with their books because it ruins the suspense, but Jesus has different goals than I do: He's removing the suspense on purpose. He wants us to see clearly where this story is heading, because he wants us to be able to work backwards from the ending into a better understanding of our role in his story now. It's a good thing, too, because the ending is not what we would have guessed. Even the glimpse he gives us shows faces full of surprise: "Lord, when...?"

LIVING WITH THE END IN VIEW

God's system for measuring success is not like ours. It's striking that on the day of judgment, Jesus is not going to be looking for how much access we've had to the halls of human power and influence. He'll be more interested in how accessible we've been to people in the halls of pain—places like hospitals and prisons and cold streets and broken homes and wherever the tears are falling and needs are pressing.

He won't be counting our fame and followers, either. He wants to see us treat others well. He made those people. Every one of them. And he has a particular interest in how we behave towards the ones who can offer nothing in return. Our treatment of them is a clear test of whether or not we really know and understand God's love for us—the love he gives freely in Jesus, even though we have nothing to offer him in return except our need for a Saviour.

Our treatment of the "least of these" is also the test that most clearly demonstrates what kind of dreams we are pursuing with our lives. Is our primary goal to climb as high as possible on the ladders of human success? If so, then that will be shown in how the people around us—and above and below us—become tools for us to use, steps for us to climb on in our quest for personal glory. The reality of this may be disguised in our relationships with the rich and influential, because we need their favour to help us advance, but it will come out clearly in how we treat the people we cannot find a way to gain advantage from.

However we justify it, whatever we say about it, whatever Scriptures we quote about it, the real test comes down to what we actually do unto the people who cannot do unto us. As Jesus' brother James puts it, "Religion that God our Father accepts as pure and faultless is this: to look after orphans and widows in their distress and to keep oneself from being polluted by the world" (James 1:27).

The normal way to do things on this planet is to handle people with great care if they have power and privilege, lest we offend them and lose the advantage of their good opinion. That same care does not usually apply to people we consider beneath us, though. In those cases, it is generally acceptable for us to brush them aside and ignore them, speak harshly to them, or use them for our own purposes.

Their good opinion won't help us climb the ladders of success, and treating them badly may provide a signal to those around us that our own status is higher than theirs, because we can use or abuse them and they can't do anything about it. Yes, it is a signal—but the people around us are not the only ones seeing it. Our Creator is also watching. It may be that no one else in the world notices how we mistreat his handiwork, but he notices. He takes it personally: "I was hungry and you gave me nothing to eat, I was thirsty and you gave me nothing to drink, I was a stranger and you did not invite me in, I needed clothes and you did not clothe me, I was ill and in prison and you did not look after me".

I AM THE LEAST OF THESE

When I see my fellow humans in the kinds of situations Jesus spoke of, I should see the image of their Creator reflected in their faces, and know that as I serve them, I am serving him as well. I should also see a reflection of myself: I was the hungry and thirsty one, unable to satisfy myself with anything the world has to offer apart from God. I was the stranger who had rejected my own Creator and isolated myself from him. I was the naked soul, with nothing to cover my guilt. I was the one mortally sick with sin and unable to escape the prison of my own destructive desires.

This is where Jesus found me, and instead of ignoring me or condemning me as hopelessly beneath him, he invited me to his feast of life. He satisfied me with "rivers of living water" (John 7:38), welcomed me into his own family, and covered my guilt with his own righteousness. He healed my sick soul and set me free to live the life I was made to live. And what is the life I was made to live? It is a life of knowing, enjoying, and imitating my Saviour, a life of loving him and loving the people he loves by giving myself for their good out of the never-ending wealth of all that God has given to me.

My deepest needs for forgiveness and life have been met in my Saviour, and the same is true for anyone who comes to him. Every person in the world needs this life more than anything else the world has to offer. Every person in the world is eligible for God's eternal feast, if they will only come. But how will they know that unless someone tells them (Romans 10:14)? How could we ever withhold from anyone their invitation to God's eternal feast of life? There is no greater gift we could ever give, and no gift that is more needed. But very often people have immediate practical needs too—sometimes they need dinner. Or a winter coat. Or someone to visit them in prison and remind them that their life matters. By providing these things, we could be the ones to give them an appetiser of the life and love that they can find in God. Real love does not seek only one kind of good or another: spiritual or physical, eternal or temporal—it seeks all good, always. For everyone.

As long as you live on Earth there will be real needs all around you. Everyone everywhere needs the gospel; but physical needs like the ones Jesus spoke about are everywhere as well. Maybe they are in the areas of town you drive through without thinking about the people you're driving past. Maybe they are behind the closed doors of neighbours whose actual reality does not match their immaculately cultivated facade. One thing is certain: the needs are nearby. If you do not see them, it is not because they have ceased to exist. It is because your eyes are pointed in the wrong direction. All you need to do is look.

OPENING OUR EYES

When our church looked, we discovered a refugee centre a few minutes from our comfortable houses, with no shortage of needs. Some residents were falling sick from poor nutrition, and God provided the resources we needed to begin delivering fresh fruit regularly. We've also been able to provide vitamins and baby supplies, do Bible studies, help with immigration paperwork, and give dozens of Bibles to people who asked for them. I know of other churches who looked and now they share meals and holidays and Bible studies with international university students, far from the support networks of home. Others looked and started providing support groups for drug addicts, or supplies to women in crisis pregnancies, or meals and coats for the homeless, or safe houses for victims of trafficking or abuse. There is never a shortage of needs. There is always a shortage of people willing to do something about them.

This is so normal that we are often inured to it, but that doesn't make it right. In our world, it's normal to live on the rung we've achieved on the ladder of success, enjoying its benefits and looking up to our next promotion, our next step towards the heights of prominence and power and privilege, without ever pausing to think of the real, living people around us and below us. No one expects us to widen our social circle to include the people who are considered beneath us—but if we can somehow snag the attention of someone above us, then our own status will rise from our proximity to them.

No one has to teach us about any of this. This is the way the world works. This is why suburbanites don't hold BBQs with anyone but suburbanites, and the established folks don't reach out to the new arrivals, and the penthouse club doesn't shoot pool with the cleaning staff. This is why some churches that are careful about their theology are not careful about problems like drug addiction or pornography, because problems like that are beneath them and people with problems like that are beneath them, too. It's all so familiar, so intuitive. It's all so wrong.

What would it look like for us to turn this entire system over? To look—really look—and see that the people the world around us considers beneath us are the same ones that the God above us considers precious? What would it look like for us to leverage whatever station we have attained not to attain more for ourselves but to joyfully give to others, especially those who cannot give in return, in the pattern of our Saviour? Jesus said that if you did it for them, "you did it for me". That's how much God values the people that the world overlooks. It's hard for us to imagine, and hard for us to remember, but it's true, and it changes everything. For example, it might change the seating in church, as the book of James says:

"My brothers and sisters, believers in our glorious Lord Jesus Christ must not show favouritism. Suppose a man comes into your meeting wearing a gold ring and fine clothes, and a poor man in filthy old clothes also comes in. If you show special attention to the man wearing fine clothes and say, 'Here's a good seat for you,' but say to the poor man, 'You stand there' or 'Sit on the floor by my feet,' have you not discriminated among yourselves and become judges with evil thoughts?" (James 2:1-4)

Is it possible that a church who meets in the name of Jesus could refuse their own Saviour a seat? It is, because their Saviour is the one who said "Whatever you did not do for one of the least of these, you did not do for me". Unfortunately, the people of God do not always use his measuring tools when assessing the value of others. I wonder how much our churches would change if we did use them, consistently? What would it look like to value equally the homebound and the toddlers and the caretakers and the pastors and the single mothers and divorced fathers and the successful businessmen and talented vocalists and the non-verbal children with special needs and what would it look like to value each and every one of them fully, the way Jesus does? Would our priorities and ministries change? Would our budgets change?

These attitudes don't begin with institutions. They begin with hearts that have tasted the love of God for hopeless strangers like you and me. God opened the door of heaven to desperate sinners like us, and we follow him by welcoming others the same way. My great-grandfather did this at the door of the YMCA. You can do it, too, by opening your door, and your table, to people who don't fit well in your comfortable social circle. You can bring hope to someone who feels forgotten in prison, or in a nursing home, or standing on the edge of the room with no one to talk to. You can bring encouragement to someone suffering in a hospital bed, or grieving a loss, or missing the life they left behind as they try to find their way in a place they don't understand. You can give your money, or your life, to help strangers around the world receive their invitation to God's eternal feast of life. You can cross the invisible lines of society like your Saviour, and give out of all that he has given you. You can look—really look—and see the value of the "least of these" who are being ignored or put down by others, but never by their Creator.

When the Son of Man comes in his glory, and spreads his feast of life, will he thank you for having him over for dinner?

SMALL DREAMS IN BIG SUCCESS

Inner-city Chicago, 1970s: The door opened on the lift, and my grandfather, Robert Peach, headed for his office in the Sears Tower, the tallest building in the world. This son of Horace Peach had worked his way up to become the manager of the Quality Control Division at Sears, Roebuck & Company, the largest retailer in the world. Actually, he created the Quality Control Division. By doing so, he became one of the founding fathers in a global movement to establish quality standards worldwide. He wrote books that helped companies implement the new standards, and worked with the World Bank to bring quality-management training to developing nations.

But Bob Peach didn't believe that he was inventing anything new. He saw the fundamental principles of quality control as a reflection of the character of God, and he simply applied that to his industry, just as he applied his knowledge of God's generosity to his personal finances. He had experienced God's generous grace, so he became generous, too. So much so that his accountant once asked, "How can I put down this much giving on your taxes? No one will believe it!" This was true: the IRS didn't believe it, so they audited him. But the giving was real.

Bob and his wife Shirley lived in an ordinary house in an ordinary neighbourhood, in contrast to the impressive homes of his colleagues. Their goal in choosing a home wasn't to impress others. They had a different goal: their first priority was to find a faithful church that was reaching out to others, where they could grow and serve God alongside faithful believers. They found this in a small church on the west side of the city, and intentionally picked a home nearby. Maybe people weren't impressed by the house, but they were served there—usually food, and sometimes a place to stay, if needed. It could be a powerful foreign politician, or a friend from church, or a factory worker who was new to the area—it didn't matter, all were treated to the same open door, the same open table, and the same listening ears and open hearts.

On the surface, the life my grandfather lived looked quite different from the life my great-grandfather spent at the door of the YMCA. Measured with the normal tools of the world, it was bigger in every way—more successful, more powerful, more influential, more wealthy, and more memorable. A closer look at the two men tells a different story, though. It is a story of shared goals and a unified direction, but in different circumstances. Horace leveraged his low position at the YMCA to serve hopeless strangers on the streets. Bob leveraged his high position in Sears to serve people around the world by helping set quality standards, while at the same time investing his wealth in gospel ministry at home and abroad, and investing his time in the individual people and needs he saw around him.

In different ways, this father and son both built their lives and their work on the same priority: a love for God that drew them to give their lives in service to his eternal kingdom first, above anything else that the world could offer them. One man intentionally stayed low on the ladders of human success, because he wanted to serve others who were low in the eyes of the world, yet highly valued in the kingdom of God. The other reached a high place by the world's measuring systems, yet he kept his big success focused on the same small dreams: love for God, and love for the people God loves.

As I look back at the life of my grandfather, I see the difficulty of his commitment. In a world driven by money, power and fame, it is never an easy task to keep your life focused on God's priorities. Jesus himself said, "It is hard for someone who is rich to enter the kingdom of heaven" (Matthew 19:23). If you succeed in a big dream, like my grandfather did, that success will always come with built-in temptations: to forget your dependence on the God who made you, to forget your place in his larger story, and to focus on creating your own great and memorable legacy. You will be tempted to forget the value of the people around you who have not reached the same rung on the ladder of success, or forget the value of realities that don't register on those ladders, like character, integrity, and self-sacrifice.

THE GOD OF YOUR DREAMS

Robert Peach did not forget who he was or what God had made him for. He did not build his ambitions around his success in the Sears company hierarchy, or shape his decisions around their priorities. It's a good thing, too: he lived long enough to see the dramatic fall of the Sears retail empire. He saw the iconic tower, where his office had once been, being bought out, renamed, and surpassed by the height of the Burj Khalifa skyscraper in Dubai. But his dreams survived, because they were not tied to that tower, or the height of his position inside it.

His dreams began in the small, quiet space of each new morning, before the meetings and decisions and drama of the day, in his private communion and conversation with his Creator. He knew God was King of the universe, and recognised him as King of his dreams as well. It was there, in the unnoticed, unapplauded habits of prayer and meditation on God's word, that my grandfather's dreams were born. It was there that he saw through the noisy promises of dreams that look big here and now, and small in eternity. It was there that he remembered the big, lasting value of things the world considers small, like a close relationship with God, a character shaped to reflect Jesus, and a love for people—including people who couldn't help him climb the ladder of success.

My grandfather's life showed me that big success can be built on, and focused on, the small dreams that matter most. His example helps me take stock of my own dreams, and where they are coming from, and where they are going. That's an important practice, because dreams, especially big ones, can be deceptive. Minds are adept at justifying whatever hearts say they want. The best of intentions can change course over time in the chaos of a thousand daily choices, and the focus of my dreams can shift, unnoticed, from God and everything he is, to me, and everything I want for myself right now. I don't think I'm the only one who struggles with this. Are you dreaming and working your way towards big success, higher positions, more money, or a wider following online? If so, the most important question is not how big you become, or how much you succeed. The most important question about your dreams is where are they coming from, and where are they going?

Are your big dreams built on God, or on your own desires for value, significance and happiness? Are you aiming them towards his kingdom, or towards your own goals of becoming more loved, or more important, or more satisfied? Big dreams can never bring you the lasting value, significance and happiness you long for. And they don't need to. You already have value as God's creation, loved and honoured and sought-after. You already have significance being a character in God's story. And if you have come to God through Christ, you already have access to the joy of knowing and loving, and being known and loved, by your Saviour. If you think that achieving a big dream can win you more than God has already given to his children, think again. I don't care how big your dreams are, you won't be able to out-do God. So build your dreams on him.

No other dream can compare with being close to God himself. If you lose everything else, but keep him, you'll still have more than everything the world can offer you. When a rich young ruler came to Jesus and asked what he should do to inherit eternal life, Jesus told him to give away everything, and follow him. That man had made money his god. He was trying to satisfy his desires with wealth and power and influence, and Jesus knew he couldn't keep those things and also follow him. Maybe some of us can't, either.

Jesus said you cannot serve both God and money, and that goes for everything else, too—you cannot serve both God and influencer status, or God and career success, or God and a good reputation, or God and anything else. When it comes down to it, there is only room for one king on the throne of your heart. If big success (or dreaming of big success) pulls your attention away from God, it's not worth it. Full stop. If you see this happening in your own heart, or if your friends see it and love you enough to warn you, then it may be best for you to give up your big dream for the sake of the greater treasure of knowing God. "What good will it be for someone to gain the whole world, yet forfeit their soul?" (Matthew 16:26).

RICH YOUNG RULERS CAN HAVE SMALL DREAMS, TOO

The rich young ruler needed Jesus more than he needed big success. We all do. But not every rich young ruler is called to give up their success like he was. There are times when God calls his people to follow him and live for his kingdom in the middle of success the world measures as big. One such example is William Wilberforce, who was rich, young, and a ruler in the British government. He wanted more than anything to follow Jesus, so he asked his friend John Newton (author of the hymn "Amazing Grace") if he should step down from the government to serve God. Newton advised him to step up and serve God in the government. This is exactly what he did, and which is why, eventually, the British government abolished slavery.

The point is not that big dreams, powerful positions, wealth or fame are evil. The point is that none of these things are the end goal. If Wilberforce had made power his god, he would have leveraged it to gain more power, and held on to it for as long as possible. Instead, he made many powerful enemies by taking a stand for what was right. He leveraged his own power to serve the "least of these", turning the ladder of success upside down and making it his ambition to lift those he found at the bottom, instead of rising higher himself. He did not give up his power, but he also did not let it have control over him. In a world of politics so often defined by personal gain, he kept his dreams focused on faithfulness to God and love for people—especially the people that everyone around him considered too small and insignificant to care about. The irony is that today there is a huge statue of Wilberforce in his hometown, but only historians know the names of most of his self-serving contemporaries. And a statue is nothing compared to the honour of standing before God himself and hearing him say, "Well done, good and faithful servant! You have been faithful with a few things; I will put you in charge of many things. Come and share your master's happiness!" (Matthew 25:21).

Wilberforce got the statue, but he got it because the statue was never his goal. His goal was faithfulness to God, and good for others, and this is success—whether there is a statue at the end of it or not (there usually isn't). Statues are temporary, anyway. Opinions change. Memories fade. But the approval of God is for ever. The point is never how big our dreams are, or how successful we are in reaching them. The point is always to love God and love people— the two greatest commandments, according to Jesus.

DREAMS WITH DIRECTION

If you achieve dreams the world considers big, make sure they are built on dreams the world considers small. Let your dreams—whatever their size—be born in the quiet, close fellowship of your own relationship with your Creator. Jesus said, "Let anyone who is thirsty come to me and drink. Whoever believes in me, as Scripture has said, rivers of living water will flow from within them" (John 7:37-38). Come to Jesus and fill your thirsty soul every day with the life that only he can give you. Drink in his word and his promises, bring him your thanks and praise and your requests. Learn from him what is true, what is precious, and what is worth the investment of the life he breathed into you. Be filled, and then let his love and generosity overflow out of your satisfied soul and into the thirsty world around you.

They will overflow, because God's love and generosity are too much to contain in yourself alone. When God fills you, your dreams naturally begin to flow out of his provision towards his priorities. The size they reach and attention they attract is not nearly as important as this origin, and this direction. So look at your life, right now: Are your dreams flowing out of your relationship with God? Are they running towards his priorities?

You can answer these questions by looking at the time you spend with God, and at how you are using the influence and resources he has already given you, big or small. Are you leveraging the assets he has blessed you with for the sake of God and others, or are you using them to gain personal advantage over others? What do you spend your money on? Where do you invest your time? What do you use your phone for? Some people think they will serve God better when they have more of the things they want, or more of a margin, or a better safety net, or something along those lines. The reality is that if you cannot be faithful with the small things you have right now, you will not be faithful with the big things you don't have (Luke 16:10).

One of the primary ways this faithfulness will show up is in your relationships to those who are closest to you, like your family, your local church, and your community. Paul said that people who ignore their family responsibilities have "denied the faith" (1 Timothy 5:8). These are the people who see your life for what it really is, not just a soundbite of your wisdom or a picture of your success. If you do get to serve large crowds, that service will always be limited in its depth. Your service to people close to you will not. This is the level where God's kingdom grows best—like a plant that grows quietly from a seed (Matthew 13) benefiting from the repetition of small daily things like sunshine and rain. In the same way, God's people grow in the repetition of daily things like forgiveness, encouragement in the truth, and obedience. If you miss this, any big dreams you achieve will be hollow. It would be better to miss the big dreams.

Remember that God is already working around you in more ways than you can imagine, developing the plot of his big story towards his glorious conclusion. You do have a role in the story. But does that mean you need to be the one to start a big new initiative or that your name needs to be recognised by millions? Maybe. That might be the role God has for you. If it is, don't reject it. But then, it's also possible that you might be able to serve people better by getting involved in things that are already happening, things other people have already started, or things no one else pays much attention to. You might not get as much applause that way, but whose kingdom are you building, anyway?

However high you climb, however wide your influence becomes, or great your power grows, your goal should always be to imitate Jesus' humility and service, as we see in Philippians 2. That's what the apostle Paul did. As one of the most influential men the world has ever known, he told us in Romans 15:20 that "it has always been my ambition to preach the gospel where Christ was not known". His ambition was not to make himself known; it was to make Christ known. Paul did not think that people needed to know more about Paul. He wanted them to know Jesus. His love for God taught him God's love for people, and that love drove him to give everything he had for their good, to the glory of God, like his Saviour before him. He refused to measure himself with the metrics of worldly success (2 Corinthians 10:12). Instead, he threw everything he had into priorities that don't even register on those measuring systems, and he never looked back:

"But whatever were gains to me I now consider loss for the sake of Christ. What is more, I consider everything a loss because of the surpassing worth of knowing Christ Jesus my Lord, for whose sake I have lost all things. I consider them garbage, that I may gain Christ and be found in him." (Philippians 3:7-11)

Paul's ambition was aimed directly at Jesus. To the world around him, he looked like a fool, seeking the approval of God, not people, and risking everything to pour himself out in service "like a drink offering" (Philippians 2:17) for others instead of looking out for number one. No matter how big his dreams became, they were built on, and pointed at, things that the world considers small. My grandfather did the same in his high position, just like my great-grandfather before him, in his low position. Are you aiming your dreams at Jesus, and letting him set your priorities? The size your dreams reach will never be as important as what they are built on, and what they are pointed at.

SMALL DREAMS,
BIG EFFORT

As the runners gathered at the starting line of the 1983 Sydney to Melbourne ultramarathon, it was obvious that one of them was not like the others. The other athletes were kitted out with expensive equipment and detailed plans for how they would tackle the 875 kilometre (543 mile) race. Cliff Young, a 61 year-old farmer, showed up in overalls and work boots. When questioned by a curious reporter, he said, "I grew up on a farm where we couldn't afford horses or four-wheel drives, and the whole time I was growing up—until about 4 years ago when we finally made some money and got a four-wheeler—whenever the storms would roll in, I'd have to go out and round up the sheep. We had 2,000 sheep on 2,000 acres. Sometimes I'd have to run those sheep for two or three days. It took a long time, but I'd catch them. I believe I can run this race."

For the next five days, he ran. Kind of. Most witnesses describe it as more of a "shuffle". It was not fast. At the end of the first day, the crowd of professional athletes were far ahead of him. Then, after 18 hours of running, they stopped to rest, but Cliff kept going. He shuffled on and on, and barely slept at all. In the end, he shuffled all the way to the finish line—a full 10 hours ahead of the next contestant. He said afterwards that he had imagined he was chasing after sheep and trying to outrun a storm.

You could say that Cliff didn't train for the race, but you would be wrong. His whole life was training. Chasing sheep is hard work, even if it's not the kind of work most people notice or applaud. Cliff Young had spent his life on things the other contestants probably considered irrelevant, but they didn't think that at the finish line. In a similar way, the work you put into small dreams may go unnoticed by the world around you. You may not gain attention or applause for it. But when the finish line of life comes, the hard work you put into loving God and others now will pay off, more than you or anyone around you today can imagine. Jesus said:

> *"Whoever wants to be my disciple must deny themselves and take up their cross and follow me. For whoever wants to save their life will lose it, but whoever loses their life for me will find it. What good will it be for someone to gain the whole world, yet forfeit their soul? Or what can anyone give in exchange for their soul? For the Son of Man is going to come in his Father's glory with his angels,*

and then he will reward each person according to what they have done." (Matthew 16:24-27)

The paradox of living is that those who run hard to win their own life will lose everything in the end, no matter how big their pile of winnings is, while those who give up their lives to run after God and the dreams he made them for will run straight into the arms of life himself—"I am the way and the truth and the life" (John 14:6) Jesus said, because life is a person, not a thing. The closer we are to Jesus, the more we experience his promise in John 10:10: "I have come that they may have life, and have it to the full". That's why the writer of Hebrews tells us to "throw off everything that hinders and the sin that so easily entangles" so that we can "run with perseverance the race marked out for us, fixing our eyes on Jesus, the pioneer and perfecter of faith" (Hebrews 12:1-2). Jesus is the one who planned this race for us, the one who gives us the strength to run it, and our greatest prize at the finish line.

This is not the same dream that the world around us is running for, so it follows that the way we run won't look like the way they run. That doesn't change the fact that running is hard work. Cliff Young may not have been a conventional racer, but there's nothing easy about rounding up 2,000 sheep on 2,000 acres before the storms roll in. That man had endurance and determination, in the extreme, built up over decades of intensely hard work. No one recognised his life of ordinary farm labour as race training, but his lifestyle had prepared him for the race better than any of the professionals' training programmes had. Cliff Young didn't add race training on top of the rest of his life; he simply lived every day and every year and decade of his life in a way that made it possible for him to show up on race day and win an ultramarathon. As we run the race towards God and the dreams he made us for, we should "run in such a way as to get the prize" (1 Corinthians 9:24)—not as a checklist of training exercises added on top of our already busy lives, but rather as a complete lifestyle directed towards faith and obedience and love for God and others.

ADDING AND SUBTRACTING

This will not be easy. Small dreams require big effort. Pursuing them with everything we've got will reshape our lives both negatively and positively. Negatively, because our focus on small dreams will mean that other things in our lives get less attention. Humans are limited, and we can't pursue everything at the same time. Positively, our commitment will require us to be intentional about building the rest of our lives towards the dreams God made us for.

Negatively, a commitment to small dreams could mean that you have to set aside some dreams to pursue others. My brother did this when he decided not to accept a promotion at work that would have required more travel, because he had small children at home and he wanted to be present to invest in them. Usually it's a good idea to accept a promotion, but he knew that he didn't have the time or space to pursue both dreams at the same time. Maybe later he will. But there could be times when you have to make a definite choice between big and small dreams. If big dreams are asking you to compromise your integrity, they are asking too much. If they are demanding that you do things that could harm others, they are too costly. You need your integrity more than you need a job at a prestigious company that requires dishonest reporting. You can't love others well by launching your acting career with a role that glorifies unfaithfulness, dishonesty and selfishness. Don't sacrifice small dreams for big ones. Your dreams might get bigger that way, but what good will they do?

Choices like these are hard. They feel like a kind of death, and for good reason: they are. A part of us really is dying, a part we loved and treasured, and dying never feels good. But remember: "Whoever loses their life for my sake will find it". There is life on the other side—real life: full of real love, real freedom, real joy and real satisfaction, as well as purpose and meaning. So if it comes to a choice, don't let big dreams change your course.

On the positive side, a pursuit of small dreams will also mean that we build new things in to our lives, like an athlete who spends time in the gym every day and eats healthy food, or like a sheep farmer who gets up early to feed his animals and chase them in before the storms. How can you direct the details of your life towards small dreams? Let's think about how that might look in a few areas.

YOUR SCHEDULE

What does it look like when God's priorities set the schedule? For Jesus, it looked like taking regular time to get away on his own for prayer, spending plenty of time with his disciples, and going out of his way for people like "tax collectors and sinners" (Matthew 9:10-13) who were definitely "the least of these" in the social hierarchy of the time. Are you investing time in your relationship with God, in your family and local church, and in others— especially those who are being overlooked? It's no good saying that you love God and agree with him about the things that matter most if you don't actually spend time with God or the people he loves.

I don't mean once in a while. Runners who only run once in a while don't do well. Christians who only talk to God once in a while don't, either. And when it comes to loving others, remember that time invested repetitively into the same people becomes more powerful. A cup of coffee to encourage a friend in need is more effective when it is built on years of shared life and accumulated trust. A hot dinner for a homeless stranger meets a need, but it takes time to fix the part about them being a stranger, and more time to sort through whatever it was that made them homeless in the first place. Showing up at church and smiling at each other is nice, but those smiles mean a lot more when you've put time into carrying each other's burdens, wiping each other's tears, and reminding each other of God's truth through the many highs and lows of real life. Jesus didn't give his disciples a weekend seminar to tell them everything they needed to know before he went to the cross. He shared his life with them for years. Who are you sharing your life with?

There are also a handful of choices in life that will shape your schedule for years, or decades. Big decisions like education, career, marriage, family, where to live, and how to spend your retirement. When you come to making these choices, what factors will you weigh up? Will you think mostly about how much money you can make, how much pleasure you can experience, how much social prominence you can win, or how large your name will be written in the annals of history? Or will you consider instead how you can invest your time and your dreams in the priceless, eternal treasures that only come from knowing God and loving the people he loves? As we saw in the last chapter, these small dreams can shine through the big ones, so there's no formula here—but there is a direction. The direction is down in service, and the emphasis is on priorities and people that the world usually considers small.

YOUR SKILLS

Some people are better at starting races, others at finishing. Some are best with long distances, others with short. The best athletes will know their strengths, and leverage them fully, like Cliff Young shuffling through the night. They will also know their weaknesses, and do what they can to compensate for them. If you want to run the race God has marked out for you well, it will help you to do the same. But be careful here—when we measure our strengths and weaknesses, it's very easy to start comparing those to other people around us. I told you in chapter 1 that I'm an "all-rounder", which means that my best abilities are usually quite ordinary when compared to others. Maybe you're different, and your best is better than anyone's. Either way, that's not the point.

The important question is not, "Who's the best?" The important question is, "What are these abilities for?" If you develop your skills to increase your own status and win the approval of others, then yes, it matters if you're better at things than they are. But if your talents are aimed at small dreams, then your goals will change: instead of working to outperform others to prove your own relative greatness, you can work instead to help them reach their full potential and find their place in the big story God is writing. Sometimes they might rise above you in the metrics of success. Great! It's not a competition. You can celebrate their success, and keep lifting them, and keep lifting others, any way you can. This is a point Paul made in 1 Corinthians 12, when he wrote about believers working together as the body of Christ. Competition for personal glory in the body of Christ is like an auto-immune disease where the body fights against itself. We have better things to do.

The best way to avoid this kind of trouble is to avoid measuring your abilities against the abilities of others in the first place. Measure them instead by how they can help you reach the small dreams that matter most. If you enjoy cooking, you could develop that skill and use it to leverage the massive power of hospitality. You don't need a Michelin star for that. If you are naturally good at languages, maybe you could learn to communicate well with immigrants in their mother tongue. A talent for sports could connect you with people in your community, or give you the opportunity to help children grow through coaching, or provide you a platform to become an example of living for God instead of personal glory. If you're highly organised, you might be able to help your local church minister more effectively and efficiently. The possibilities are almost endless.

You don't have to be the best. Mostly, you just need to show up willing to work. I have a friend in Alabama who got an award for doing legal work for a local charity. He said, "A lot of people could have done it". This is true, I'm sure. The thing is, they didn't. The charity didn't need people who *could* do the job. They needed someone who *would* do it. He did it well, but if a job is worth doing, then it's worth doing adequately, if that's all you can manage. It's also worth investing the time and effort it takes to learn to do it better. Get the training you need. Get the gear that helps. Leverage your talents for good at the highest level of excellence you can reach, and don't let weaknesses stop you from doing what needs to be done. In all of it, remember that the path to eternal glory leads down in service. How can your skills help you achieve small dreams?

YOUR TO-DO LIST

When I think of working towards small dreams with my schedule and skills, there's always one big never-ending problem that seems to get in the way: the to-do list. I don't know what your to-do list has on it, but I know you have one (at least mentally, if not physically), and I know it's filled with plenty of everyday jobs like meal prep, laundry, mowing, paperwork, taxes, dishes, shopping, cleaning, and of course the tasks of your day job. These monotonous, repetitive demands feel almost pointless, just a series of annoying interruptions that only block us from pursuing our real dreams. The never-ending to-do list never stops sucking our precious, limited time and energy into jobs that will just need to be done all over again tomorrow. Can your small dreams survive the constant invasion of distracting necessity?

Yes. If your dreams are to love God and others well, then you'll find that the constant demands of normal life are not distractions at all—they are opportunities. A home with regular dinners and clean clothes can be a tangible, repetitive expression of God's care and provision for his children. A job well done, however monotonous it may feel, can be a repetition of his constant work on behalf of the world he made.

Just think: he's been feeding the birds and watering the plants the exact same ways for the entire history of the world, without once complaining or quitting because it got boring. He must not be tired of work like this, because he uses the same template for his eternal kingdom, comparing its growth to the growth of an insignificant-looking mustard seed (Luke 13:18-19).

Jesus taught his disciples to ask God to "give us today our daily bread" (Matthew 6:11). This shows us that God is not above doing daily chores for his children. He is constantly tending his world and his people with the quiet, consistent, repetitive work of a patient gardener or a shepherd caring for his flock. Most of our opportunities to display his kind of love and sacrifice for others will come on this level as well, in the repetitions of ordinary daily work. This even includes the interruptions and to-do lists that make up so much of our lives. The to-do list is not a barrier in our way. It is full of ways to run hard after small dreams.

YOUR SWEAT

I've used running as an example here because it's a good one, and because it's used in the Bible. But I don't particularly like running. It's hard work. It makes me sweaty. I'd rather walk. But when it comes to my life, I believe God made me for more than a leisurely stroll through the time he is giving me on Earth. Yes, there are times for rest, and there are so many good gifts to enjoy along the way, but there is also a prize to run for, and it's worth the hard work involved in the running.

Living our lives against the current of the world will never be easy. Pouring ourselves out in service for God and others in the details of real life and real relationships will be messy and tiring. If we give ourselves in service to others, some of them will thank us, but others will not. Some won't even notice what we do for them, and others may start to think of our service as their right, as if we were their servants. Just look at how people treated Jesus, and how they still treat him today.

Just look at how Jesus responded. He kept going, no matter what people said, or what difficulties he had to face, because he knew where he was going, and he knew why. He even "endured the cross, scorning its shame" and he did it, "for the joy that was set before him" (Hebrews 12:2). He knew the story of redemption and restoration that he was writing was worth the work and sacrifice. Your part in the story is worth it, too. It's worth the hard, daily work of loving God with your time, serving others with your talents, tending God's world with your labour, and investing everything you've got into God's eternal kingdom.

SMALL DREAMS,
BIG REWARDS

"Sell the furniture? *All* of it? But what will we sit on? How will we live?"

Her eyes shot daggers at her husband. Had he gone insane? He had been his normal, sensible, hard-working self when he left for work that morning. Now he was raving like a lunatic about selling everything they had to buy a useless piece of land!

"Who cares about the furniture?" he said, "We'll need to sell the house, as well. And the car. Would that be enough...?" She dropped her fork. She couldn't help it. He didn't notice. "Maybe we can pawn our wedding rings..."

"Stop it." (She was proud of how firm and controlled her voice sounded.) "You're scaring the children. If you're trying to make a joke, you've crossed the line. It's not funny."

"I'm not joking, dear." His face told her this was true, and she shuddered in spite of herself.

"But you're wrong about that field—it may not look like much, but it's not useless. There's treasure buried there! I found it today while I was working. So much of it—you wouldn't believe it, really I could hardly believe it myself, but it's there. Don't worry, no one else saw it, I covered it back up before they came." His words were spilling out fast in his excitement. "If we can scrape together enough money to buy that field, the treasure will be ours! All of it! Then we'll have everything we could ever need, and so much more. This treasure is more valuable than everything we have, everything we could ever have. We're rich—rich beyond our wildest dreams—and all we have to do is give up everything we have!"

Jesus said, "The kingdom of heaven is like treasure hidden in a field. When a man found it, he hid it again, and then in his joy went and sold all he had and bought that field" (Matthew 13:44).

The kingdom of heaven is not a kingdom of sour self-sacrifice, long-faced long-suffering, or dour duty. The kingdom of heaven is a kingdom where people do backwards things, things like giving up everything they have, and they do it out of pure, overflowing, unstoppable joy! Why? Because everything you have is nothing compared to the untold riches of heaven. Because giving everything in service to God and the bigger story he is writing is no loss if you're already secure in your identity.

There is a never-ending abundance in being an adopted child—and heir—of the eternal King of kings and Lord of lords, the Creator and owner of all things, the awesome all-powerful Saviour victorious over sin, death, suffering, tears and pain, the winner of life, the fountain of living water, the merciful and gracious giver of every good gift, for ever and ever, amen. He is, himself, the greatest treasure in the universe. And he has given himself to bring us back to himself, if we will only trust him and follow him.

What else do you want? A Ferrari that wears out as you use it? A title that someone else will claim as soon as you're gone? A bigger sitting room with a better view and designer couches? Are you kidding? Who cares about the furniture? You can have the great, eternal treasure of heaven. How can any amount of earthly wealth compare? How can earthly fame compare to heaven's honour? How can earthly power compare to the privilege of reigning with Christ (2 Timothy 2:12)? The things you have here and now can never last—even your life on Earth is short. But Jesus said it is possible for you to invest your life and everything you have into eternal treasures that cannot be destroyed. He said it is possible to "store up for yourselves treasures in heaven" (Matthew 6:20), which means that your investments in his kingdom now, no matter how unnoticed they are by people, are producing a reward that is better than anything money can buy on Earth. Jesus said that those who are faithful with the small things God has entrusted to them on Earth will be given greater responsibility in the kingdom of heaven (Luke 19:17). He said that those who humble themselves in service, like he did, will be exalted to high honour in his kingdom, like he was (Matthew 23:11-12). It doesn't have to look big to the world. It doesn't have to register on their ladders of success. Their ladders aren't going to last, anyway.

It's no wonder people throughout history have counted everything else a loss compared to knowing and serving God. It's why my great-grandfather Horace Peach spent his life at the door of the YMCA, welcoming strangers. It's why his son Robert leveraged success to serve others instead of using it to serve himself. It's why my friend Nancy has given away so many house keys. It's why Moses "chose to be ill-treated along with the people of God rather than to enjoy the fleeting pleasures of sin. He regarded disgrace for the sake of Christ as of greater value than the treasures of Egypt, because he was looking ahead to his reward" (Hebrews 11:25-26). These people, and so many like them, caught sight of dreams that were better than anything they could dream for themselves, and they never looked back. Their lives became a reflection of their Saviour's life of downward service and sacrifice for God's story of redemption, flowing freely from the confidence of knowing who they were in Christ and where their service would lead.

That's why the apostle Paul said, "Even if I am being poured out like a drink offering on the sacrifice and service coming from your faith, I am glad and rejoice with all of you. So you too should be glad and rejoice with me" (Philippians 2:17-18). Do you see what he did there? He said, *I am suffering. Rejoice with me!* Which is not the way people normally talk—unless they know that their suffering has a purpose, and a reward that is greater than anything they have lost. Paul, Nancy, Horace, and countless others throughout history, found the treasure in the field, and in their joy, they gave everything they had to gain it. And like the man in Jesus' story, their joy came immediately, even before the treasure was fully grasped.

FINDING THE TREASURE

The same joy is available to you. It is a joy not tied to circumstances, but overflowing out of the treasure of Christ. Which means that your happiness does not have to depend on anything going according to your plans—it can come instead from the deep satisfaction and confidence of being part of God's plans. This confidence is the soil where true contentment grows. As Paul says, "I have learned the secret of being content in any and every situation, whether well fed or hungry, whether living in plenty or in want. I can do all this through him who gives me strength" (Philippians 4:12-13). He says that if we are in Christ, then nothing, not anything "will be able to separate us from the love of God that is in Christ Jesus our Lord" (Romans 8:39). And he says that this security is the ground where peace can finally overcome anxiety:

> *"Do not be anxious about anything, but in every situation, by prayer and petition, with thanksgiving, present your requests to God. And the peace of God, which transcends*

all understanding, will guard your hearts and your minds in Christ Jesus." (Philippians 4:6-7)

Contentment. Satisfaction. Joy. Peace. Purpose. Meaning. Love. Aren't these the things that big dreams were supposed to give us? They are, but the big dreams were never big enough to keep their promises. When Jesus turned the ladder of success upside down, he showed us that the treasures we've been seeking, and so much more beyond them, are hidden in a field—hidden in his mustard-seed kingdom that grows in the ordinary daily things of ordinary life, the things that the world keeps overlooking as insignificant. We thought the answers were above us, that somehow if we made ourselves big enough then we could mean something, and be recognised, and finally be satisfied. But looking up and climbing over each other to make ourselves as big as possible has only led us away from the very things we were seeking.

I'm sure the man who found that treasure in the field had worked hard to build up his possessions and position in life. But the moment he saw real treasure hidden in the dirt, nothing else mattered. Everything that had held his attention before gave way to one singular focus: he had to have that treasure. I'm sure his neighbours thought he had gone crazy as they watched him sell all the things he had worked so hard to collect for himself. Then to see him take everything he had and buy a regular old field—it had to look like he was giving up in the race to success, like he had lost sight of what was valuable. What they didn't see is that he had discovered the truth about where value was actually located.

So it is with the treasures of heaven: they are won by those who look down and get their hands dirty in the ordinary fields of ordinary life, who happily pour their time and energy and resources into seemingly small acts of love and faithfulness because they see immeasurable value where others see nothing worth noticing. They see that the person who is least on the ladders of success is more precious than a chance to live on the top rung. They see that serving that person is serving God himself. They see that drawing close to God is better by far than being treated like him by others. They see that having a small part in his story is greater than the best story they could ever write for themselves. They see the treasure, and in their joy, they give everything they have for dreams that the world considers small.

FINDING FREEDOM

This is freedom. I know it doesn't look like the freedom most people talk about, but that's only because it's better than they can imagine. So many people today demand autonomy, and value independence above almost everything else, because they think that the only path to personal fulfilment is to define their own dreams, and then pursue them, and reach them. In other words, they see freedom in terms of being able to collect the possessions and positions and such that will give them the meaning and happiness they seek. They are like a man who saw treasure in a field but kept walking because he didn't really think it was worth much, and anyway he likes his furniture and he's working to get more of it. The Bible has a different word for this way of life: slavery— because "people are slaves to whatever has mastered them" (2 Peter 2:19).

The highway of personal autonomy is really the path of slavery to dreams that can never keep their promises, work that can never bring lasting satisfaction, and applause with no power to grant real worth or significance. When Jesus came, he turned this whole system around by freely giving us, in himself, everything we had been working so hard to find without him. He showed us that true freedom is not found in independence, it can only be received in dependence on him. Jesus said, "If the Son sets you free, you will be free indeed" (John 8:36). Free.

Free from the nagging fear that everything you are and everything you do on this dust speck in the stars is too small and too insignificant to mean anything.

Free to accept and enjoy the love of your Creator, without having to deserve it.

Free to generously give the same love to others, even when they don't deserve it, knowing that God's love for you can never run dry.

Free from the guilt and shame of sin, through the forgiveness of God.

Free to forgive others who wrong you, out of the forgiveness you've received.

Free from the impossible pressure of having to write your own legacy, create your own purpose, and define your own destiny.

Free to take up your place in the great epic of salvation history, in the role you were carefully designed for.

Free to risk your reputation, comfort, security and even your life, for the sake of a story that is larger than you are.

Free to use the ladders of success to reach down and lift others instead of climbing to secure your own worth.

Free to notice, and befriend, and love other people who can't help you climb higher in the opinions of others.

Free to live above the opinions of others and their systems of measuring value and success.

Free to receive praise without letting it define you or forget how small you are.

Free to receive criticism without letting it define you or forget how loved you are.

Free to enjoy your life for what it is right now without having to perfect it.

Free to push hard for change where it is needed, in the confidence of the victory Jesus has already won, and will complete.

Free to look pain and sorrow and ageing and tragedy in the eye, confident that none of them can destroy your meaning or your reward.

Free from basing your worth in your productivity, your beauty, your level of success, or the size of your dreams.

Free to pursue the treasure in the field, in the small dreams others may see as pointless.

Free indeed.

DREAM SMALL

You don't have to wait for anything to dream small. You don't have to prove your skills or make a team, or pass an interview, or put together a portfolio, or anything of the sort. Jesus already did all the work required to forgive you and bring you back to God, so all you have to do is trust him and listen to what he says about what is valuable and how he made your life to work. Obedience to God, faithful service to others, humility, sacrifice—these things may not look like treasure to the people around you, but don't worry about what they think. Don't worry about the furniture, either, or any other dream you might have to let go of. God made you for more than the biggest dreams on Earth can give you.

You are here for a purpose. You were carefully crafted with a perfect plan in mind. You are a character in the greatest story ever told, and your life, and your actions, and your decisions—even today—can send shockwaves into eternity. Maybe the role God has for you is big and public. Maybe it is quiet, behind the scenes, where hardly anyone will notice. Don't worry about that. You can invest in loving God and loving the people he loves from wherever you are, and the best ways to do that have always been the closest, most ordinary, most overlooked and under-appreciated ways, like humble service to humble people and time spent with God and all the little ways we can remind each other of God's truth and God's love and the big story he made us to be part of.

Right now, today, you can dream small in your work, focusing your effort on honouring God and benefitting the people he made in his image. You can dream small at home, in the slow and steady repetition of provision and service and love. You can dream small by investing in your local church, leveraging your gifts to serve Christ's body on Earth. You can dream small by spending time in God's word and prayer, alone and with other believers, soaking God's love and truth into your soul and receiving the strength you need to live the life he made you for. You can dream small by cleaning the toilets for your family, looking after a sick relative made in God's image, listening to a friend, helping a stranger, seeking out the unpopular, giving money, giving time and attention, giving your strengths and talents and your weakness and ordinariness and whatever else you have for God and his kingdom of people he loves.

Don't settle for less. "Run in such a way as to get the prize" (1 Corinthians 9:24). "Throw off everything that hinders and the sin that so easily entangles" (Hebrews 12:1) and don't look back. Fix your eyes on Jesus, the pioneer and perfecter of your faith, who formed you for his story before you were born and wrote all your days in his book. "Make it your ambition to lead a quiet life" of faithfulness and love for God and others (1 Thessalonians 4:11). Find the treasure in the field. Find the joy of turning the ladders of success upside down.

Dream small.

BIBLICAL | RELEVANT | ACCESSIBLE

At The Good Book Company, we are dedicated to helping Christians and local churches grow. We believe that God's growth process always starts with hearing clearly what he has said to us through his timeless word—the Bible.

Ever since we opened our doors in 1991, we have been striving to produce Bible-based resources that bring glory to God. We have grown to become an international provider of user-friendly resources to the Christian community, with believers of all backgrounds and denominations using our books, Bible studies, devotionals, evangelistic resources, and DVD-based courses.

We want to equip ordinary Christians to live for Christ day by day, and churches to grow in their knowledge of God, their love for one another, and the effectiveness of their outreach.

Call us for a discussion of your needs or visit one of our local websites for more information on the resources and services we provide.

Your friends at The Good Book Company

thegoodbook.com | thegoodbook.co.uk
thegoodbook.com.au | thegoodbook.co.nz
thegoodbook.co.in